AUGUST'S
WORKBOOK TO ACCOMPANY
NURSE ASSISTING
THE COMPLETE GUIDE

Lisa Rae Whitley, RN, ADN
Candace S. Weinzinger, RN, BSN
Dr. Carrie L. Jarosinski, RN, CNE, CWP

August's Workbook to accompany Nurse Assisting: The Complete Guide
Lisa Whitley, RN, ADN; Candace S. Weinzinger, RN, BSN; and Dr. Carrie L. Jarosinski, RN, CNE, CWP
© 2023, August Learning Solutions

Published by August Learning Solutions
Cleveland, OH

August Learning Solutions concentrates instructors' efforts to create products that provide the best learning experience, streamlining your workload and delivering optimal value for the end user, the student.

www.augustlearningsolutions.com

All rights reserved. This book or any portion thereof may not be reproduced or used in any manner whatsoever, including but not limited to photocopying, scanning, digitizing, or any other electronic storage or transmission, without the express written permission of the publisher.

Print ISBN: 978-1-941626-59-7
EPUB ISBN: 978-1-941626-60-3

Printed in the United States of America
27 26 25 24 23   1 2 3 4 5 6 7 8 9 10

Textbook activity answers, instructor resources, test bank questions, workbook answer keys, and skills videos are available to professors via the Instructor Portal. Contact your CSR or support@augustlearningsolutions.com for access.

Cover image credits: iStock.com/ElenaMedvedeva and August Learning Solutions

This book was written based on current information and healthcare guidelines. Please note that federal and state guidelines and/or certification requirements may differ from those in this book. Instructors and readers are responsible for adhering to federal, state, and employer guidelines and regulations when teaching and performing care.

The Publisher, along with the authors and reviewers, assumes no liability for the application of the content found in this book.

Contents

Chapter 1: Healthcare Yesterday and Today   1

Chapter 2: The Nursing Assistant Role: Where You Fit In!   7

Chapter 3: Communication and Documentation   13

Chapter 4: Professionalism and Ethics   19

Chapter 5: Body Structures and Functioning Processes   25

Chapter 6: Common Diseases and Disorders   29

Chapter 7: Infection Control Practices   33

Chapter 8: Body Mechanics and Workplace Safety   37

Chapter 9: Reducing Client Injury and Falls   41

Chapter 10: Restraints and Restraint Alternatives   45

Chapter 11: Basic First Aid Measures   49

Chapter 12: Holistic Care of Clients   55

Chapter 13: Client Room Environment   61

Chapter 14: Preventing Skin Breakdown   65

Chapter 15: Bedmaking   71

Chapter 16: Positioning, Moving, and Transporting Clients   75

Chapter 17: Ambulation, Restorative Care, and Adaptive Equipment for Clients   81

Chapter 18: Vital Signs   87

Chapter 19: Bathing   91

Chapter 20: Grooming   95

Chapter 21: Nutrition   99

Chapter 22: Elimination and Specimen Collection   105

Chapter 23: Care for the Client with Dementia and Cognitive or Mental Health Challenges   111

Chapter 24: Oxygen Therapy and Respiratory Interventions   117

Chapter 25: Care for the Medical and Surgical Client   123

Chapter 26: End-of-Life Care   129

Name _____

Chapter 1: Healthcare Yesterday and Today

1.A Matching Definitions

_____ 1. Chronic illness
_____ 2. Co-pay
_____ 3. Medicaid
_____ 4. Almshouses
_____ 5. Infectious illness
_____ 6. Client
_____ 7. Consumerism
_____ 8. Managed care organizations
_____ 9. Healthcare premium
_____ 10. Medicare
_____ 11. Deductible
_____ 12. Consumer of healthcare
_____ 13. Outpatient surgery
_____ 14. High deductible health plan

A. Places for the homeless, poor, elderly, or insane to stay

B. A consumer of healthcare who uses any part of the healthcare system

C. A specific dollar amount or percentage that must be paid by the individual for each healthcare service received

D. A certain amount of money each year that the individual must pay for healthcare services before the insurance company will start to pay for any services used

E. Occurs when a germ enters the body and causes sickness

F. Insurance programs that worked to reduce the rising healthcare costs in the United States

G. Health insurance plan for people with low income and the disabled; funded though federal and state taxes

H. Gives access to health insurance for older adults and, in certain cases, the disabled; funded through federal taxes

I. The belief that consumers drive choice, leading to increased choices offered

J. Anyone who accesses healthcare or interacts with a healthcare agency or provider

K. A condition or disease that people live with for a long period of time

L. A surgical procedure that does not require an overnight stay

M. The cost that the individual must pay every month toward their healthcare plan; usually taken out of the client's paycheck if employed

N. An insurance plan with a higher deductible than a traditional plan; generally, a lower monthly premium, but the individual will pay more health care costs before the insurance company starts to pay

Name _____

1.B Reflective Short-Answer Exercises

Jennifer is a 32-year-old who comes to the urgent care clinic with increasing shortness of breath due to asthma. Because they can't afford the deductible on their insurance plan, they haven't seen regular doctor. Instead, they tried treating their symptoms with an herbal remedy they read about on the Internet. The doctor at the urgent care clinic has now ordered two new prescriptions to fill at the pharmacy. Jennifer states that they will not be getting the medications because they cannot afford them.

1. How would Florence Nightingale help Jennifer?

   _____
   _____
   _____
   _____

2. What is preventing Jennifer from seeking medical care?

   _____
   _____
   _____
   _____

3. Is continuing to visit the urgent care clinic the best way for Jennifer to treat their asthma?

   _____
   _____
   _____
   _____

4. Is continuing to go to urgent care for an acute problem cost effective? Why or why not?

   _____
   _____
   _____
   _____

1.C Fill in the blanks using terms found in the word bank.

quality of life	heart disease	Medicare
arthritis	poor	assisted-living facilities
inflation	home care	competition
respectful	injured	sick
managed care organizations	infectious illness	

1. Florence Nightingale portrayed the art of nursing through her compassionate care of the _____, _____, and _____.

2. A(n) _____ occurs when a germ enters the body and causes sickness.

3. Two examples of chronic illnesses are _____ and _____.

4. _____ changed the way doctors and other healthcare providers were paid for their services.

Name _____

5. The rate of healthcare costs is growing faster than that of _____.

6. The root of consumerism in today's healthcare system is _____.

7. _____ may be an option for a client who needs healthcare services but chooses to remain in their own environment.

8. _____ may not offer round-the-clock skilled nursing care.

9. You must be _____ of the alternative choices made by your client.

10. The _____ plan gives access to health insurance to older adults and to some younger people with certain disabilities.

11. Your role as a nursing assistant today is to ensure that the _____ for our client is the best it can be.

1.D Multiple-Choice Exercises

1. Florence Nightingale was able to show a connection between the spread of infection and unsanitary conditions with the use of
   a) doctor questionnaires.
   b) handwashing studies.
   c) statistics.
   d) patient interviews.

2. Florence Nightingale believed it was important to consider the patient's
   a) ability to pay.
   b) family background.
   c) medical history.
   d) environment.

3. An example of a chronic illness would be
   a) measles.
   b) diabetes.
   c) pneumonia.
   d) chicken pox.

4. Patients staying at an almshouse were at risk for
   a) an increased number of infectious diseases.
   b) violent crimes.
   c) becoming mentally ill.
   d) a high number of medical accidents.

5. Health insurance as a standard of American life was developed
   a) after the Great Depression.
   b) after the Korean War.
   c) after World War II.
   d) before World War II.

6. Medicaid is a
   a) state-supplemented health insurance plan for clients age 65 or older.
   b) federal health insurance plan for clients over age 65.
   c) group insurance partially supplemented by employers.
   d) state-supplemented health insurance plan for clients with disabilities or low income.

7. The payment that a client gives their healthcare provider for services before the insurance begins to pay is called a
   a) deductible.
   b) healthcare premium.
   c) co-pay.
   d) managed care fee.

8. In the 1800s, there was a notable decrease in infectious illnesses due to
   a) an increase in almshouses.
   b) the start of group insurance.
   c) a rise in specialty healthcare providers.
   d) the use of public health interventions.

Name _____

9. The rising cost of healthcare is partly due to the
   a) use of MCOs.
   b) increase in chronic diseases.
   c) increase in infectious diseases.
   d) use of Medicaid insurance.

10. A consumer of healthcare who uses any sector of the healthcare system is called a
    a) provider.
    b) patient.
    c) resident.
    d) client.

11. Managed care organizations (MCOs) have led to a(n)
    a) increase in consumer options.
    b) shorter hospital stays.
    c) rise in healthcare costs.
    d) increase in consumer knowledge.

1.E Choose the best response to the following scenarios.

1. Your neighbor is in need of skilled nursing care. Their daughter asks you to explain the difference between long-term care and home care. The best response would be
   a) that long-term care is most appropriate for a client who requires ongoing treatment around the clock.
   b) that home care is available only to clients who have a lot of money.
   c) to tell the daughter it would be best if they could move in and care for her mother.
   d) to tell the daughter to call her mother's doctor.

2. Your client has been recently diagnosed with a serious illness and has been searching the Internet for information. Your client is upset and tells you the information gathered regarding their illness says that they will die. The best response would be to
   a) tell the client to prepare funeral arrangements.
   b) inform the client that they should only read medical websites.
   c) instruct the client to contact their healthcare provider to further discuss any concerns.
   d) help the client search online for healthcare services.

3. A client you have been caring for in the nursing home tells you they are going home. They will be receiving care from a home health agency and are not sure what to expect. You should tell the client
   a) that you need to get your supervisor, who will give them more information about what to expect from their home health provider.
   b) that nursing home care is much better than home health care.
   c) not to worry and that everything will be fine.
   d) you know other clients who have been very happy with home health services.

4. You are caring for a client who comes from a different background than you do. You do not agree with the client's beliefs and lifestyle. Following Florence Nightingale's example, how will you care for this client?
   a) Try to convince the client that they are wrong and you are right.
   b) Care for the client without regard to background, class, or wealth while putting your personal opinions aside.
   c) Ask the nurse to convince the client to change their ways.
   d) Refuse to care for the client because you do not agree with them and have nothing in common with them.

Name _____

5. You now have health insurance and have recently been treated by the doctor for a medical condition. You receive the bill in the mail and are confused because you are being charged for a portion of that treatment. What will the insurance company tell you when you question this?

   a) Your treatment was expensive, and an additional fee was added.
   b) You are paying for services you did not use.
   c) You may be paying for your neighbor's treatment as well.
   d) You have not met the deductible on your plan and are required to pay for a portion of the medical services.

6. A client in your facility is upset to hear that the medication the doctor has ordered is not the same medication that they had read about in a current magazine. The appropriate response for the nursing assistant would be to

   a) immediately tell the nurse of the client's concerns.
   b) inform the facility's Director of Nurses.
   c) ask the client to explain and then report this to the nurse.
   d) let the other nursing assistants know so they do not upset the client.

This page intentionally left blank.

Name _____

Chapter 2: The Nursing Assistant Role: Where You Fit In!

2.A Matching Definitions

_____ 1. Hospice
_____ 2. RCAC
_____ 3. CBRF
_____ 4. Acute care facility
_____ 5. Joint Commission
_____ 6. Scope of practice
_____ 7. Chain of command
_____ 8. Ombudsman
_____ 9. Respite care
_____ 10. Assisted-living community
_____ 11. Long-term care facility
_____ 12. OBRA
_____ 13. Delegated task
_____ 14. Resume

A. Services that provide a safe environment for older adult clients or developmentally disabled clients over the age of 18

B. A volunteer who helps to protect the rights of residents by investigating complaints or reports of violations of resident rights

C. Offers care for residents needing skilled nursing care for a long period of time

D. Offers specialty end-of-life care for clients who have less than 6 months to live

E. A healthcare facility that provides short-term care for clients who have an immediate illness or injury

F. A facility that is comparable to senior apartment living and that offers minimal care

G. Legislation that mandated many regulations regarding the care of residents, resident rights, and the training requirements for nursing assistants

H. An entity that accredits and surveys most acute care facilities in the United States; formerly known as JCAHO

I. A facility that bridges the gap between living independently and living in a healthcare facility such as a nursing home

J. One type of assisted-living community

K. A job or action that a supervisor asks you to complete either verbally or through a written care plan

L. The responsibilities, skills, and actions that you are permitted and expected to follow after you have completed your training

M. A hierarchal route of communication from one member of the healthcare team to the next

N. A one-page summary of your personal, academic, and professional accomplishments

Name _____

2.B Reflective Short-Answer Exercises

Steve just started working in a nursing home. Their previous job was as a personal care worker at an assisted-living facility. Even though they are comfortable caring for clients, they find working at the new facility challenging and often confusing.

1. How are nursing homes and assisted-living facilities different from each other?

   _____
   _____
   _____
   _____

2. Why is Steve struggling in their new job at the nursing home?

   _____
   _____
   _____
   _____

3. How is taking care of the same type of client different in various settings?

   _____
   _____
   _____
   _____

4. Do regulating bodies make a difference in the nursing assistant's job duties? If so, how?

   _____
   _____
   _____
   _____

5. What could Steve have done differently on their first day at the nursing home to make it easier?

   _____
   _____
   _____
   _____

Name _____

2.C Fill in the blanks using terms found in the word bank.

home health aides	hospice	Omnibus Reconciliation Act
Medicare	dying	refuse
acute care	scope of practice	chain of command
reinforce	assisted-living facilities	document
provide personal care		

1. One of the primary duties of a nursing assistant is to _____.
2. Part of your responsibility as the nursing assistant is to understand your _____.
3. _____ are designed to bridge the gap between living in a healthcare facility and living independently.
4. _____ may shop or run errands as well as provide daily caregiving.
5. A(n) _____ facility is one that provides short-term care to clients who have an immediate illness or injury.
6. Nursing homes are regulated by the _____.
7. _____ is often used as payment for home health care, which is usually a temporary service.
8. Once a task is completed, the nursing assistant must _____ what was done.
9. _____ is often used in the military setting and also works well in healthcare.
10. The goal of _____ is not to cure, but to assist the client and family with the _____ process.
11. After the initial teaching is done by a nurse, the nursing assistant can _____ what has been taught to the client.
12. The nursing assistant must _____ a task that is not within their scope of practice.

2.D Multiple-Choice Exercises

1. The most expensive type of healthcare setting is usually a(n)
    a) assisted-living community.
    b) hospice organization.
    c) respite care facility.
    d) acute care facility.

2. OBRA is federal legislation that regulates
    a) rehabilitation hospitals.
    b) long-term care facilities.
    c) respite care services.
    d) home health agencies.

3. To ensure that hospitals are in compliance with federal regulations, they are surveyed by the
    a) Joint Commission at least every year.
    b) Joint Commission at least once every 3 years.
    c) Accreditation Commission for Healthcare every 6 months.
    d) Healthcare Quality Association every 2 years.

Name _____

4. A nursing assistant who works for a long-term care facility would most likely be caring for a resident who

   a) needs 24-hour care due to their dementia.
   b) had heart surgery 2 days ago.
   c) needs supervision and activities while their family is shopping.
   d) needs assistance only with medications and meals.

5. Respite care offers services for clients who need

   a) rehabilitation and extensive therapy.
   b) a safe environment for short periods of time.
   c) end-of-life care.
   d) close monitoring of vital signs.

6. You are a new nursing assistant and work well in a fast-paced, changing environment. You might enjoy working

   a) on the medical-surgical floor at a local hospital.
   b) at a skilled nursing facility (SNF) with dementia care.
   c) at a chiropractic clinic assisting with exercises.
   d) at a nursing home that offers hospice services.

7. A nursing assistant working in a long-term care facility is likely to work with

   a) public health department staff.
   b) activity and dietary aides.
   c) physician assistants.
   d) radiologists and radiology technicians.

8. Scope of practice for a nursing assistant includes

   a) checking a client's blood sugar level.
   b) giving clients their ordered medications.
   c) removing a urinary catheter.
   d) offering emotional support to a hospice client.

9. A task that is NOT in the scope of practice for a nursing assistant is

   a) delivering medications.
   b) providing dementia care.
   c) assisting with daily living activities.
   d) aiding with basic personal care tasks.

10. You have noticed that one of your clients is more agitated and upset after starting a new medication. You should report this to the

    a) director of nursing.
    b) charge nurse.
    c) client's healthcare provider.
    d) client's partner.

11. The care plan for one of your clients states that they are to have their back brace applied before they are to get out of bed in the morning. You are unsure how to do this, so you should

    a) ask one of your coworkers to do it for you.
    b) have the client tell you how they normally wear it.
    c) explain to the nurse that you do not understand the directives.
    d) have the nursing assistant from the previous shift apply it before they leave.

12. It is in the nursing assistant's scope of practice to

    a) educate a client on a new diet.
    b) remind the client to perform their leg exercises.
    c) show a client how to put on their wrist brace for the first time.
    d) instruct a client on how to take a new medication.

Name _____

2.E Choose the best response to the following scenarios.

1. A hospice agency is looking for a nursing assistant to work on the night shift. During your interview for the position, you are asked to describe your best qualities. How should you respond?

    a) No qualities are needed because on the night shift everyone is sleeping.
    b) I am compassionate, empathetic, and have emotional strength.
    c) I am nice, quiet, and easy to work with.
    d) I don't work well with others, so I like the night shift.

2. Your client in the assisted-living facility can no longer stand and needs more help than the staff can provide. The client's daughter is very upset and asks you why their mother is being transferred to a long-term care facility. How should you answer them?

    a) Ask them to please wait while you get the supervisor who can explain the situation in more detail.
    b) Inform them the facility is short staffed most of the time and cannot properly care for their mother.
    c) Tell them you're not sure but whatever the reason their mother will be well cared for.
    d) Politely ask them not to ask you these types of questions because you do not make the decisions.

3. During the sixth week of your new hospital job, you realize the fast pace and constant demands are too difficult. How should you speak with your supervisor regarding these concerns?

    a) Tell the supervisor that you prefer to be assigned only clients whom you feel comfortable caring for.
    b) Ask your supervisor to assign the other nursing assistants some of your tasks.
    c) Ask your supervisor if you can talk about other opportunities available in the facility that could be a better fit for your personality type.
    d) Tell your supervisor that you could do a better job if given more rest periods during your shift.

4. The nurse you are working with asks you to perform a task that is not within your scope of practice. What is your best response?

    a) Tell the nurse that if they give you written instructions, you will perform the task.
    b) Politely remind the nurse that the task is not within your scope of practice.
    c) Inform the nurse that you are going to the director of nursing to report them for asking you to do something that is not within your scope of practice.
    d) Tell the nurse that you cannot perform the task, but you can find a nursing assistant who will.

5. While caring for a client in the nursing home where you work, a doctor enters the room and gives you instructions on how to properly care for the client's heel wound. What is your best response?

    a) Listen carefully and report to the nurse the instructions given to you.
    b) Tell the doctor to please write the information down and that you will give that to the nurse when they return.
    c) Ask the doctor to wait while you get another nursing assistant because two sets of ears are better than one.
    d) Inform the doctor that you are the client's nursing assistant but that you would be happy to find a nurse to assist them.

6. Your home health client asks you to explain the proper instructions given by the doctor regarding their recent hospital stay. What is your best response?

    a) Tell them you that are unable to give initial instructions but that you will call your supervisor.
    b) Instruct the client to go online and find the proper information.
    c) Tell them that you will call the doctor and have them explain the instructions.
    d) Tell the client that you will call their daughter and let them explain.

Chapter 2 • 11

This page intentionally left blank.

Name _____

Chapter 3: Communication and Documentation

3.A Matching Definitions

_____ 1. Receptive aphasia
_____ 2. Medical abbreviation
_____ 3. Nonverbal communication
_____ 4. Subjective data
_____ 5. Oral reporting
_____ 6. Empathy
_____ 7. Communication disorder
_____ 8. Incident report
_____ 9. Objective data
_____ 10. Medical error
_____ 11. Therapeutic communication
_____ 12. Verbal communication
_____ 13. Data
_____ 14. Expressive aphasia
_____ 15. Electronic Health Record
_____ 16. Autism

A. Expressing ideas or information through the use of speech

B. Information that cannot be measured; a feeling or opinion

C. The use of body language and facial expressions to convey ideas or emotions

D. A communication disorder that can make It difficult to understand the spoken language.

E. A document that is filled out to describe a specific occurrence of exposure or accident that led to, or had the potential to lead to, an injury

F. To have understanding and compassion for others

G. A mistake made by a member of the healthcare team before or while providing care

H. Information that can be measured; an object or action that is observed

I. A way of combining active listening skills and acknowledging feelings

J. Verbally conveying information to another member of the healthcare team

K. A shortened medical word or group of words

L. A speech or language problem that results in impaired interactions with others

M. A communication disorder that can make It difficult to produce words or to speak clearly.

N. Pieces of information

O. A neurological disorder that impairs communication and social interaction

P. The digital version of a client's paper chart, making information available instantly and securely to authorized users.

3.B Reflective Short-Answer Exercises

Margaret is a nursing assistant assigned to care for Mrs. Grey, who is on a strict NPO diet. During caregiving, Mrs. Grey complains of a dry mouth, and asks if they can have some ice to moisten their mouth. Margaret gets them a glass of ice chips. Thirty minutes later, Mrs. Grey is nauseous, has an emesis, and says their stomach hurts. Margaret gets their vital signs, which are all in the normal range.

1. NPO stands for "nothing by mouth." Based on this, what did Margaret do wrong?

2. How could the medical error have been prevented?

3. Should Margaret have asked the nurse to clarify or explain their directions?

4. What should Margaret have said to the nurse when asking for clarification? Be specific.

5. What is the objective data that Margaret should report to the nurse?

6. How should Margaret have communicated the NPO status—and the need to follow it—to Mrs. Grey?

7. If Mrs. Grey was upset about their NPO status, how should Margaret have reacted?

3.C Fill in the blanks using terms found in the word bank.

care plan verbal communication subjective data
Standard system nonverbal communication objective data
military time acquired hearing loss
milliliters training medical abbreviations
oral report language lives
incident report aphasia metric

1. Mistakes in healthcare can cost _____.
2. _____ is a feeling or hunch.
3. A statement that is measurable or a fact is _____.
4. A(n) _____ is given to your supervisor or another member of the healthcare team, usually at the end of the shift.
5. Expressing information or ideas through speech is called _____.
6. Reducing the use of _____ will help decrease the number of medical errors.
7. The _____ is a form that is supplied by the facility for documentation of an accident or exposure.
8. Liquid volumes are typically documented in _____, but sometimes cubic centimeters are used.
9. When speaking with a client who has _____, make sure that they can see your face.
10. Body language and facial expressions are forms of _____.
11. The Imperial System of measurement is sometimes referred to as the _____.
12. A communication disorder is a speech or _____ problem that results in impaired interactions with others.
13. Communication disorders can either be congenital or _____.
14. Always request _____ on new equipment before assisting your client.
15. Clients may suffer from expressive or receptive _____, which means that either the client is unable to speak or to speak clearly, or the client is unable to understand spoken language.
16. The _____ is a tool created by the nurse to communicate what the nursing assistant needs to do to safely care for a client.
17. Measurements of smaller weight units in healthcare are most often noted in the _____ system.
18. _____ is based off a 24-hour cycle.

3.D Multiple-Choice Exercises

1. The nurse informs you that Mrs. Jones needs to have their HS snack. You are unsure what time you should be giving the snack. You should

    a) ask one of the other nursing assistants.
    b) look it up in the dictionary.
    c) ask the nurse for clarification.
    d) give the snack as soon as it comes from the kitchen.

2. Using fewer medical abbreviations means that

    a) nurses use fewer abbreviations in their oral reports.
    b) abbreviations aren't used when doctors write orders.
    c) there is a decrease in healthcare errors.
    d) medical errors are eliminated.

3. You think Mr. Thao has a sore throat because they are refusing to eat their breakfast. This is an example of

    a) objective data.
    b) subjective data.
    c) therapeutic communication.
    d) evidence-based information.

4. When you attempted to feed Mrs. Johnson their lunch, they became very upset and said, "I don't want any of this! I want to lie down! Leave me alone!" When reporting this, you tell the nurse that Mrs. Johnson

    a) doesn't have an appetite.
    b) was too tired to eat.
    c) was angry and uncooperative.
    d) was upset and refused their meal.

5. While giving a client their scheduled shower, you notice that they have a reddened area on their back. You should

    a) report this to the nurse when you have completed the shower.
    b) report this to the nurse at the end of your shift.
    c) leave a note for the nurse at their desk.
    d) inform the client's family.

6. When discovering new information that is out of the normal range for a client, you should give an oral report to

    a) the nurse at the end of your shift.
    b) the nurse right away.
    c) the caregiver relieving you.
    d) both b and c.

7. If the nursing assistant makes an error in a paper chart, they should

    a) write the word "error" and sign.
    b) draw a line through the error and initial.
    c) use erasable ink to keep the chart easier to read.
    d) get a new sheet of paper to reduce confusion.

8. Mr. Lee is a new client at your facility. His family has just left, and you notice that they are upset and teary. When you enter their room, they say they want to go home. You should

    a) tell them that this is the best facility their family could have put him in.
    b) assure them that the staff is very kind and helpful.
    c) sit quietly with them and let them talk when they are ready.
    d) leave the room to give them privacy.

9. An example of subjective data would be

    a) a fever of 101.2.
    b) thinking a client has the flu.
    c) foul-smelling urine.
    d) a client reporting pain at level 4.

10. Melissa is a client with severe hearing loss. They have an assistive listening device that they use with their hearing aid. You are not sure how to use their listening device. You should

    a) ask Melissa how to use the device and hearing aids.
    b) get another nursing assistant to help you with Melissa's care.
    c) request training on the listening device before helping Melissa.
    d) ask Melissa's family to show you how to use the device.

Name _____

11. Judah has a hearing deficit from working in construction for many years. This is an example of

   a) a congenital hearing loss.
   b) an acquired hearing loss.
   c) a neurological disorder.
   d) expressive aphasia.

12. When communicating with a client who has hearing loss, you should do all of the following EXCEPT

   a) raise the pitch of your voice.
   b) speak at eye level with the client.
   c) slow your speech down.
   d) use a picture board.

13. Virgil is a client recovering from a recent stroke. They often become frustrated because they are not able to understand your directives. This is an example of

   a) receptive aphasia.
   b) expressive aphasia.
   c) congenital hearing loss.
   d) an emotional deficit.

14. You are charting an incident that occurred at 6:30 that evening. When documenting, you should write that time as

   a) 6:30 PM.
   b) 06:30 PM.
   c) 1830.
   d) 18:30.

15. When caring for a client with expressive aphasia, you should

   a) speak slowly and clearly.
   b) use short, direct sentences.
   c) use a picture board or book.
   d) talk in a normal pitch of voice.

16. One ounce of fluid equals

   a) 30 cc.
   b) 30 mL.
   c) 10 mL.
   d) both a and b.

3.E Choose the best response to the following scenarios.

1. You make a mistake while charting in a paper record. The appropriate action to take is to

   a) erase the mistake the best you can.
   b) use correction fluid to cover the mistake.
   c) draw a single line through the mistake and initial.
   d) ask the supervisor to correct the document for you.

2. You enter your client's room and find them grimacing and holding their stomach. The best response is to

   a) assume they need to use the restroom.
   b) ask them if they are OK and be prepared to assist if needed.
   c) tell the nurse they are in pain and need medication.
   d) come back later when they are feeling better

3. You are on your way home after working the night shift when you realize you forgot to document on one of your clients. The appropriate action to take is to

   a) call the facility and report to your supervisor as soon as possible.
   b) do nothing because you are tired after working all night.
   c) decide to chart the next time you work.
   d) call your coworker and ask them to chart for you.

4. You discover skin tears and bruises on one of your home health clients. You should

   a) call the client's son and update them on the injuries.
   b) ask the client what happened, document, and update your supervisor immediately.
   c) call 911.
   d) treat the injuries and then call 911.

Name _____

5. You are having trouble communicating with your hearing-impaired client, and they are becoming upset and frustrated. What should you do?

   a) Refer to their care plan to identify any communication techniques that will help you.
   b) Try sign language; you learned this in high school.
   c) Raise the pitch of your voice so they can hear you.
   d) Take a break from the client, since they are upset with you.

6. You care for a client who has expressive aphasia. How could you best care for them?

   a) Talk very slowly and use simple words.
   b) Ask simple yes or no questions.
   c) Write your directives on a white board.
   d) Ask for an interpreter.

Name _____

Chapter 4: Professionalism and Ethics

4.A Matching Definitions

_____ 1. Abandonment
_____ 2. Ethics
_____ 3. Assault
_____ 4. Negligence
_____ 5. Caregiver strain
_____ 6. Culturally Competent
_____ 7. Abuse
_____ 8. Informed consent
_____ 9. Misappropriation
_____ 10. Occupational Safety and Health Administration (OSHA)
_____ 11. Family Medical Leave Act (FMLA)
_____ 12. Health Insurance Portability and Accountability Act (HIPAA)
_____ 13. Culture
_____ 14. Professionalism
_____ 15. Ethnicity
_____ 16. Responsibility
_____ 17. Battery
_____ 18. False imprisonment
_____ 19. Neglect
_____ 20. Mandatory reporter
_____ 21. Law
_____ 22. Rights

A. A single or repeated action that is purposeful and meant to cause harm; can be mental, physical, sexual, or emotional

B. When caregivers emotionally can give no more to clients and start to treat clients or others poorly

C. When you can accept the differences between yourself and your client, and consider each client as a unique person

D. Principles of right and wrong that drive behavior

E. Threatening a client with physical, mental, or emotional harm

F. Refers to the national, racial, or cultural group that a person belongs to

G. When a caregiver does not follow the standards or scope of practice or the role that they are working in; they are not doing what a reasonable person would do in a given situation

H. A law that allows an employee to take a leave of absence from their job for a total of 12 weeks out of any 12-month period for certain medical needs without the risk of losing their job

I. Physically touching a client when you do not have permission to do so

J. Legislation created in 1970 that ensures that all employees have safe and healthy working conditions

K. When a caregiver walks away from their assignment before the end of the shift or before their replacement is there to relieve them, leaving clients alone and at risk

L. A privacy law created in 1996 that protects all healthcare information that can be linked to an individual, known as individually identified health information

M. The right to know what treatment options are available and the risks associated with those treatments; the client then has the right to make a choice about those options

(list continues on next page)

Name _____

N. Someone who, as part of their job, must report any abusive or unlawful activity immediately

O. Intentionally using another person's money or belongings without that person's permission

P. When a treatment or service is not provided and the client is then harmed

Q. A set of traditions and attitudes that are shared within a group of people

R. Certain beliefs or laws that determine our freedoms

S. When a client is limited from moving freely about their environment

T. Accountability for one's choices and actions

U. Working by the set of standards learned in your coursework to prepare you for employment

V. A rule that you are legally obligated to follow

4.B Reflective Short-Answer Exercises

Judy is supposed to be transferred with a mechanical lift by two nursing assistants, as delegated by their care plan. This evening, one of the CNAs chose to transfer Judy by themself because it was quicker. Judy fell during the transfer. They were transferred to the emergency room to be evaluated, where they discovered that Judy suffered a broken hip. Judy is now being admitted to the hospital for corrective surgery.

1. In the story of Judy, what information is protected by HIPAA?

   _____
   _____
   _____
   _____

2. If the nursing assistant would have explained the risks of being transferred by one and not two assistants, and Judy agreed, would this have followed informed consent standards?

   _____
   _____
   _____
   _____

3. Was the nursing assistant abiding by their responsibilities as an employee?

   _____
   _____
   _____
   _____

Name _____

4. What did the nursing assistant do when they chose to transfer Judy by themselves rather than follow the care plan?

   _____
   _____
   _____
   _____

5. What would have been the ethical choice for the nursing assistant to have made in this scenario?

   _____
   _____
   _____
   _____

6. What was the negligent action in this scenario?

   _____
   _____
   _____
   _____

7. What do you think will happen to the nursing assistant in regard to employment?

   _____
   _____
   _____
   _____

4.C Fill in the blanks using terms found in the word bank.

nurse aide registry	work ethic	time management
mandatory reporter	touching	neglect
privacy	cultural competence	leave of absence
informed consent	abuse	assault

1. _____ is a single or repeated action that is purposeful and meant to inflict harm.
2. Part of acting professionally means you have a strong _____.
3. Threatening a client with mental, emotional, or physical harm is _____ .
4. Accepting others' differences is considered _____.
5. Physically _____ a client when you do not have permission is battery.
6. _____ occurs when service or treatment is not provided and the client is harmed because of it.
7. Good _____ is a critical skill that the nursing assistant must refine in order to efficiently carry out delegated tasks.
8. A law that allows an employee to take a(n) _____ from their job is called the Family Medical Leave Act (FMLA).

Chapter 4 • 21

Name _____

9. As a nursing assistant, you are considered a _____.
10. The right to make a choice based on treatment options is _____.
11. The Health Insurance Portability and Accountability Act is a(n) _____ law.
12. The _____ is a database for employers to verify that you are a certified nursing assistant in good standing.

4.D Multiple-Choice Exercises

1. A nursing assistant becomes certified after they
   a) pass all the tests in the nursing assistant program.
   b) complete 75 hours of classroom training.
   c) pass the certification exam.
   d) finish the clinical portion of the nursing assistant class.

2. You have been assigned to an unfamiliar unit at your facility. Even though it is a new area, you ask for directives from the nurse and start your shift. This is an example of being
   a) prompt.
   b) flexible.
   c) empathetic.
   d) compassionate.

3. You are working as a nursing assistant at the local hospital when your replacement calls to say they will be late. You need to leave right away at the end of your shift. You should
   a) ask the nurse if they can call another nursing assistant to help.
   b) have the nurse work for you until your relief can get there.
   c) continue to work until your relief arrives.
   d) discuss the situation with the hospital administrator.

4. The Health Insurance Portability and Accountability Act (HIPAA) protects a client's right to
   a) control their finances.
   b) access their health records.
   c) make informed choices.
   d) keep their health information private.

5. One of your coworkers is in the main doorway of your facility when you hear them talking about a client who was especially challenging that day. The BEST response would be to
   a) join in the conversation to decrease your own stress.
   b) remind them that they should not talk about clients in a public area.
   c) let them express their frustration.
   d) report the situation to the supervisor.

6. Consumers of healthcare have a responsibility to
   a) follow the doctor's orders.
   b) make healthy choices.
   c) be respectful toward other clients.
   d) act as mandatory reporters.

7. Due to OSHA regulations, healthcare entities must provide their employees with
   a) family medical leave.
   b) inexpensive health insurance.
   c) free Hepatitis B vaccines.
   d) chicken pox vaccines.

8. One of your coworkers needs to take some time off work to take care of their sick partner. Your employer states that they have only a week of vacation available. Their BEST option is to
   a) take a family leave of absence.
   b) use the vacation days.
   c) use any sick days they have available.
   d) resign from their position after giving a 2-week notice.

Name _____

9. You suspect that one of the other nursing assistants has been verbally abusive to one of your older clients. The best response would be to

   a) confront your coworker.
   b) report your suspicions to your supervisor.
   c) find out if your suspicions are right and then report.
   d) tell the client's family so they can keep them safe.

10. Using a client's phone without their knowledge is an example of

    a) invasion of privacy.
    b) caregiver strain.
    c) negligence.
    d) misappropriation of funds.

11. Jane is an older client who is unable to move on their own. The care plan states that they are to be repositioned every 2 hours. You have been especially busy, and you decide that you are able to reposition them only every 4 hours. Because of this, Jane develops a pressure injury on their tailbone. This is an example of

    a) physical abuse.
    b) battery.
    c) neglect.
    d) both a and c.

12. Sharing information or photos of your clients on your own devices or social media is

    a) allowed if the client gives permission.
    b) strictly prohibited.
    c) allowed if the client gives permission in writing.
    d) prohibited as long as you do not give the client's name.

13. You have a Native American client who wishes to have a tribal healing ceremony performed in their hospital room before going to surgery. It would involve having several people in the room. The best response is to

    a) remind the patient of the hospital's visitation policies.
    b) suggest waiting until after the surgery.
    c) report the request to the nurse.
    d) instruct the patient to discuss the request with the doctor.

14. When entering a client's room, you saw another nursing assistant slap the client across the arm. You did not report it, since it had happened only once. The person(s) who might be found guilty of abuse would be

    a) your coworker.
    b) the nurse for failing to supervise.
    c) you.
    d) both a and c.

15. The most important step in managing your time effectively is to:

    a) ask your coworkers what works best for them.
    b) decide when is the best time to take breaks.
    c) set a personal goal.
    d) ask another nursing assistant to help you complete your tasks.

16. Using a prioritized list of tasks at work leads to:

    a) proper time management.
    b) asking coworkers for more help.
    c) a chance to take more breaks.
    d) an increased workload.

17. _____ are legal documents that allow the client to state who can make choices for them in the event they cannot themselves, and what type of care they prefer to have.

    a) Verbal agreements
    b) Living wills and advanced directives
    c) Contracts
    d) Written instructions

Name _____

4.E Choose the best response to the following scenarios.

1. You are working the night shift at an assisted-living facility. Your coworker has been 20 minutes late every morning this week. You cannot leave until they get there. As a result, your kids have missed the bus. How would you resolve this situation?

    a) Tell the coworker that you are going to report them and you hope they lose their job.
    b) Remind the coworker that their shift starts promptly at 6:00 a.m. and explain why you cannot be late getting home.
    c) Talk to the other team members about how they are showing up late to work.
    d) Consistently show up 20 minutes late when you are relieving them from their shift.

2. A client asks you for a copy of their medical record. How would you respond?

    a) Tell the client that they do not have the right to their personal records.
    b) Make copies of the medical record for the client.
    c) Report your client's request to the nurse.
    d) Read the medical record to the client.

3. An older client makes sexual advances toward you. How should you respond?

    a) Tell the client that their behavior is not acceptable and report to your supervisor.
    b) Tell the client's partner.
    c) Ignore the advances.
    d) Trade assignments with your coworker to avoid the client.

4. You witness a coworker verbally abuse a client. How should you respond?

    a) Tell the coworker that it is not acceptable to verbally abuse clients.
    b) Ignore the situation; you know this coworker has a temper.
    c) Apologize to the client for your coworker's rude behavior.
    d) Make sure the client is safe and report the abuse immediately.

5. Your client appreciates the wonderful care you provide and offers you $20 as a tip. How should you respond?

    a) Gladly accept the tip for your good work.
    b) Thank the client and tell them that you cannot accept tips.
    c) Tell the client you that can accept only small tips.
    d) Split the $20 tip among your coworkers.

6. While caring for one of your clients, you notice the care plan is not correct or updated. What should you do?

    a) Pencil in the correct information.
    b) Leave it for the next shift to correct.
    c) Report your observations to your supervisor.
    d) Report your observations to the doctor.

7. Your coworker is having a hard time completing the tasks given to them, and you find yourself constantly completing your assigned tasks and a majority of theirs. How should you handle this situation?

    a) Request that your supervisor not schedule you on the same days as your coworker.
    b) Tell your coworker that you will no longer assist them when needed.
    c) Politely talk to your coworker about making a list to better organize their day and give examples of how you organize.
    d) Tell everyone else in the facility that your coworker is not a competent nursing assistant in hopes that the information will get back to them.

Name _____

Chapter 5: Body Structures and Functioning Processes

5.A Matching Definitions

_____ 1. Cardiac muscle
_____ 2. Nervous tissue
_____ 3. Organ
_____ 4. Dermis
_____ 5. Epidermis
_____ 6. Epithelial tissue
_____ 7. Integumentary system
_____ 8. Skeletal muscle
_____ 9. Smooth Muscle
_____ 10. Alimentary canal
_____ 11. Toxicity
_____ 12. Peristalsis
_____ 13. Muscle tissue
_____ 14. Hormone
_____ 15. Tissue
_____ 16. Organ system
_____ 17. Peripheral nerves
_____ 18. Cell
_____ 19. Connective tissue
_____ 20. Melanocyte
_____ 21. Subcutaneous layer

A. Nerves that send signals from the spinal cord to the rest of the body
B. The middle layer of skin
C. A chemical that is secreted to regulate body functions and emotions
D. The skin, hair, sweat glands, oil glands, fingernails, and toenails
E. A cell in the skin that makes melanin, which gives color to the skin
F. Tissue that makes movement by contracting and relaxing when stimulated; the three types include smooth, cardiac, and skeletal
G. The same type of cells grouped together; includes epithelial, connective, muscle, and nervous
H. Muscle tissue that contracts and relaxes involuntarily
I. Two or more organs working together
J. Tissue that sends and receives electrical impulses between the body and the brain
K. The outermost layer of skin
L. A type of muscle tissue that forms the heart and causes it to beat involuntarily
M. Tissue that lines our bodies inside and out; includes skin, esophagus, stomach, bowel, nostrils, trachea, and lungs
N. Consists of the mouth, pharynx, esophagus, stomach, small intestine, large intestine, rectum, and anus
O. Involuntary action of smooth muscle contracting and relaxing rhythmically; moves food and waste products through the alimentary canal
P. Tissue type that makes the body move; action is voluntary and purposeful
Q. The deepest layer of skin where adipose tissue is found
R. A type of tissue that forms a matrix that connects and supports the structure of the body; it includes blood, bone, cartilage, and fat
S. Two or more tissue types that function together
T. The smallest living unit of the body
U. Drug levels in the body that are too high

Name _____

5.B Reflective Short-Answer Exercises

Paul is an 89-year-old client living alone in their bi-level home. They typically eat only one meal a day because of poor appetite. They are on medications for their heart and cholesterol. They frequently get up at night to urinate. To get to the bathroom, they need to go up a flight of stairs. Last night on the way to the bathroom, they fell and were unable to get up off the floor due to pain in their right hip. They waited until their daughter came to check on them this morning.

1. What injury could Paul have due to their fall?

   _____
   _____
   _____
   _____

2. Why would they be unable to get up from the floor?

   _____
   _____
   _____
   _____

3. Which of Paul's aging sensory organs could have been a factor in their fall? How?

   _____
   _____
   _____
   _____

4. Could Paul's medications have been a factor in their fall? Why?

   _____
   _____
   _____
   _____

5. Which of Paul's body systems have likely been affected by age, and how could these changes have led to a fall?

   _____
   _____
   _____
   _____

Name _____

5.C Fill in the blanks using terms found in the word bank.

integumentary system	hormone	relaxes
middle layer	smallest	alimentary canal
muscle	melanin	body
organ system	contracts	

1. A cell is the _____ living unit of the body.
2. A(n) _____ is secreted within the body by one of the endocrine glands.
3. Muscle tissue _____ and _____ when stimulated.
4. A(n) _____ is when two or more organs work together.
5. The dermis is the _____ of skin.
6. The mouth, pharynx, esophagus, stomach, small intestine, large intestine, rectum, and anus make up the _____.
7. _____ gives skin its color.
8. The heart is considered a(n) _____.
9. Nervous tissue sends, transmits, and receives electrical impulses, or messages, between the _____ and the _____.
10. Skin, hair, sweat glands, fingernails, and toenails make up the _____.

5.D Multiple-Choice Exercises

1. Two or more tissue types that function together are called a(n)
   a) organ system.
   b) tissue.
   c) organ.
   d) melanocyte.

2. When the same types of cells group together, they form
   a) tissue.
   b) an organism.
   c) an organ system.
   d) epidermis.

3. Epithelial tissue forms the
   a) brain and spinal cord.
   b) heart and muscles fibers.
   c) lining of the stomach and lungs.
   d) blood and bones of the skeleton.

4. Blood, cartilage, fat, and bone are all made of this tissue type
   a) nervous.
   b) muscle.
   c) epithelial.
   d) connective.

5. One specific defense mechanism the body uses to protect itself is
   a) lining of the lungs and trachea.
   b) white blood cells.
   c) the integumentary system.
   d) lining of the sensory organs.

6. One function of the kidneys is to
   a) help regulate blood pressure.
   b) collect urine.
   c) release corticosteroids.
   d) support body metabolism.

Name _____

5.E Choose the best response to the following scenarios.

1. Your client is unable to speak. They seem agitated, are having a hard time walking, and have a grimace on their face. What should you do?

   a) Do nothing; this is common in old age.
   b) Report to the nurse these nonverbal signs of pain.
   c) Tell the next shift to be careful during ambulation.
   d) Leave them in bed for the remainder of the day to get some rest.

2. Your client is 15 minutes late for bingo and is in a hurry to get up. What is the best response?

   a) Explain to the client that it is important to move slowly from a sitting to standing position.
   b) Tell the client to hurry; bingo already started.
   c) Tell the client that it would be better not to attend bingo today.
   d) Take the client's place at the bingo table until they get there.

3. Michael is moving very slowly and taking a lot of time to complete tasks this morning. You have three other clients to care for before breakfast. What should you do?

   a) Tell Michael that you will care for them after breakfast.
   b) Allow Michael the time needed to complete the tasks.
   c) Let your coworkers care for the other three clients.
   d) Ask the nurse to reassign you to clients who can move faster.

Name _____

Chapter 6: Common Diseases and Disorders

6.A Matching Definitions

_____ 1. Hallucination
_____ 2. Stasis ulcer
_____ 3. Pressure injury
_____ 4. Orthopnea
_____ 5. Diaphoresis
_____ 6. AIDS
_____ 7. Arrhythmia
_____ 8. Aspiration
_____ 9. Benign tumor
_____ 10. Peripheral lower extremity edema
_____ 11. Fomite
_____ 12. Dyspnea
_____ 13. Kyphosis
_____ 14. Delusion
_____ 15. Dysphagia
_____ 16. Angina
_____ 17. Atrophy
_____ 18. Cystocele
_____ 19. Contracture
_____ 20. Cancer
_____ 21. Dysrhythmia
_____ 22. Malignant tumor
_____ 23. Nocturia
_____ 24. HIV
_____ 25. Metastasis

A. An ulcer that occurs from poor blood flow to the lower extremities
B. Chest pain
C. Muscle wasting
D. Excessive sweating
E. The perception of a smell, sight, sound, taste, or sensation that is not there
F. Painful swelling of the legs and feet
G. Inhaling vomit, food, or saliva into the lungs
H. The forward bending of the upper back, giving the classic hunched look of osteoporosis
I. An irregular heartbeat; also known as a dysrhythmia
J. The inability to lie flat due to excess fluid retention
K. A physical shortening of the joint ligaments
L. Shortness of breath
M. An irregular heartbeat, sometimes known as an arrhythmia
N. The need to urinate frequently through the night
O. A belief in something that is not true or supported by evidence
P. Occurs when pressure over a bony prominence is not relieved and the blood supply to that area is occluded, or cut off
Q. An inanimate object that harbors a germ or parasite
R. Difficulty swallowing
S. A prolapsed bladder
T. Human immunodeficiency virus; it targets and destroys a type of blood cell, called T cells
U. Acquired immunodeficiency syndrome; it is the end stage of an HIV infection when the body's immune system is severely damaged
V. A term used for diseases in which abnormal cells divide without control and can invade other tissues
W. Cancer that has spread or moved to other areas of the body
X. A tumor that is not cancerous
Y. A tumor that is cancerous

Name _____

6.B Reflective Short-Answer Exercises

You have been taking care of Frank in their home. You go once per week to bathe them and help out with light housework. Today when you arrive, they are still in bed, which is unusual. They smile at you, but the smile looks crooked to you. When you help them out of bed, you notice that their left side is weak and they are much more difficult to transfer than usual. When you ask Frank if they are feeling okay, Frank seems confused and is unable to answer without slurring their words.

1. What do you think Frank may be experiencing?

   _____
   _____
   _____
   _____

2. What specifically are Frank's symptoms that support your thoughts?

   _____
   _____
   _____
   _____

3. Why is it important to notify the nurse promptly when noticing these signs and symptoms?

   _____
   _____
   _____
   _____

6.C Fill in the blanks using terms found in the word bank.

AIDS	sound	shortness of breath
mental illness	physical	evidence
HIV	hunched	dysrhythmia
biopsy	urinate	atrophy
pressure injury	smell	region

1. A decubitus ulcer is also known as a(n) _____.
2. A contracture is the _____ shortening of the joint ligaments.
3. Complications associated with bed rest include blood clots, pneumonia, and muscle _____.
4. _____ targets and destroys a type of blood cell called T cells.

30 • Chapter 6

Name _____

5. A hallucination is the perception of a _____, sight, _____, taste, or sensation that is not really there.
6. A delusion is the belief in something not true or that is not supported by _____.
7. Kyphosis gives a person the classic _____ look of osteoporosis.
8. HIV will eventually progress to _____.
9. Dyspnea is also known as _____.
10. Cancer is named for the _____ or system of the body where it originates.
11. Nocturia is the need to _____ frequently at night.
12. _____ is an irregular heartbeat, sometimes known as an arrhythmia.
13. There are many causes of _____ which can include: genetics, chemical imbalances, lived experiences, exposure to drugs and chemicals, and/or traumatic injury to the brain.
14. A _____ is the removal of a small number of cells from a questionable area to test for cancer.

6.D Multiple-Choice Exercises

1. Understanding disease processes helps the nursing assistant to
   a) understand the importance of delegated tasks.
   b) care for the client in a holistic manner.
   c) identify and diagnose abnormal conditions.
   d) both a and b.

2. An example of a chronic skin disorder would be
   a) hives.
   b) psoriasis.
   c) shingles.
   d) varicella.

3. A client who is diagnosed with leukemia has cancer of the:
   a) connective and supportive tissues.
   b) bone marrow.
   c) immune system.
   d) brain and spinal column.

4. Osteoarthritis most often affects the joints of the
   a) hips, lower back, and knees.
   b) fingers and toes.
   c) shoulders and neck.
   d) arms and hands.

5. Treatment for type 2 diabetes often begins with
   a) oral medications.
   b) insulin injections.
   c) a balanced diet.
   d) eliminating desserts.

6. The highest risk factor for contracting the HIV infection is:
   a) sharing needles during drug use.
   b) multiple sex partners.
   c) unprotected sex.
   d) blood transfusions.

Name _____

6.E Choose the best response to the following scenarios.

1. You are caring for an older client who is complaining of shortness of breath. What should you do?

    a) Increase the oxygen flow on the tank.
    b) Make sure the client is safe and report to the nurse right away.
    c) Check the client's blood pressure.
    d) Take the client for a long walk.

2. Clarence is a 78-year-old client with lung disease. Clarence asks you to take them to the designated smoking area. What is the best response?

    a) Tell Clarence that you will update the nurse and then help them as instructed.
    b) Offer them a light.
    c) Tell Clarence that they are sick and should not be smoking.
    d) Take their cigarettes away.

3. You are caring for one of your home health clients when they suddenly collapse. What should you do?

    a) Call the client's doctor.
    b) Call your charge nurse.
    c) Dial 911.
    d) Ask a neighbor for help.

Name _____

Chapter 7: Infection Control Practices

7.A Matching Definitions

_____ 1. Infection control
_____ 2. Personal protective equipment (PPE)
_____ 3. Conventional capacity
_____ 4. Immunity
_____ 5. Primary prevention
_____ 6. Crisis capacity
_____ 7. Antibody
_____ 8. Germ
_____ 9. Contingency capacity

A. Preventing disease before it starts

B. Specialty equipment that acts as a barrier between the healthcare worker and infectious bodily fluids

C. A body defense against a specific germ; produced by either a vaccine or exposure to the disease itself

D. Preventing or limiting the spread of germs

E. A person will not become sick when exposed to a specific germ because of antibodies

F. Measures consisting of engineering, administrative, and personal protective equipment (PPE) controls that should already be implemented in general infection prevention and control plans in healthcare settings

G. Measures that may be used temporarily during periods of expected shortages

H. Strategies that are not commensurate with U.S. standards of care but may need to be considered during periods of known shortages

I. A microorganism that can be either a bacteria, virus, fungus, or protozoa

7.B Reflective Short-Answer Exercises

Jordan has been in the hospital receiving IV antibiotics for pneumonia. Jordan seemed to be getting better, but today they have a fever and complains of loose stools. The nurse places Jordan on contact precautions with strict hand washing. Later that day, it is confirmed that Jordan has a *C. Diff* infection.

1. What might happen to the healthcare workers taking care of Jordan?

_____
_____
_____
_____

2. What might happen to the other clients the healthcare workers are taking care of after helping Jordan?

_____
_____
_____
_____

Name _____

3. What primary prevention action could have positively affected Jordan's hospital stay?

   _____
   _____
   _____
   _____

4. Is it appropriate to hand sanitize instead of washing your hands with soap and water after caring for Jordan? Why or why not?

   _____
   _____
   _____
   _____

5. Jordan needs to have a chest X-ray this afternoon. Jordan is on contact precautions. How should you get Jordan ready before they leave their room to go to the radiology department?

   _____
   _____
   _____
   _____

6. Is there anything else you need to do before transporting Jordan? What might that be?

   _____
   _____
   _____
   _____

7.C Fill in the blanks using terms found in the word bank.

primary prevention	VRE	immunity
chain of infection	antibody	vaccine
MRSA	barrier	healthcare workers
infection control		

1. Antibodies are produced by either a(n) _____ or exposure to the disease itself.
2. _____ is preventing the disease before it starts.
3. A(n) _____ is a body's defense against a specific germ.
4. Personal protective equipment acts as a _____ between the healthcare worker and infectious agents.
5. A bodily defense that prevents illness from occurring upon exposure to a specific germ is called _____.
6. The _____ has six links.
7. _____ is preventing or limiting the spread of germs.
8. It is important for _____ to become vaccinated.
9. _____ and _____ are common drug-resistant germs in healthcare today.

Name _____

7.D Multiple-Choice Exercises

1. How a specific germ moves from one host to the next is called a

    a) reservoir.
    b) mode of transmission.
    c) portal of entry.
    d) portal of exit.

2. The MOST important primary preventative measure against the spread of disease is to

    a) eat a healthy diet and exercise.
    b) get the recommended vaccination on schedule.
    c) see a healthcare provider as soon as you become ill.
    d) wash hands or use hand sanitizer consistently.

3. The benefits of performing hand hygiene include

    a) limiting the spread of illnesses from one client to the next.
    b) reducing the risk of the healthcare worker becoming ill.
    c) controlling healthcare costs.
    d) all of the above.

4. One example of the body's nonspecific defense mechanisms would be

    a) immunizations.
    b) exposure to past illness.
    c) intact skin.
    d) wearing the appropriate PPE.

5. The MAIN reason a healthcare worker should be vaccinated against disease is that

    a) their employer offers free vaccinations.
    b) the CDC requires all healthcare workers to be immunized.
    c) vaccines help protect the worker and their clients.
    d) vaccinations need to be complete to work as a nursing assistant.

6. Hand hygiene may be done using hand sanitizer in all of the following situations EXCEPT

    a) after taking off gloves.
    b) after using the restroom.
    c) before and after eating.
    d) when coming back from break.

7. You are taking care of Esther, a client who has been experiencing loose stools. Esther is placed on contact precautions until *Clostridium difficile* can be ruled out as a possible cause of their diarrhea. When caring for Esther, you must perform hand hygiene by using

    a) soap and water after client contact.
    b) hand sanitizer before exiting the room.
    c) either soap and water OR hand sanitizer after providing care.
    d) soap and water only if your hands are visibly soiled.

8. Compared to washing with soap and water, using a hand sanitizer most often is

    a) more effective in killing germs.
    b) more time consuming.
    c) harder on the caregiver's skin.
    d) less effective against germs.

9. The PPE that a nursing assistant must wear when taking care of a client is based on the

    a) client's abilities and needs.
    b) nursing assistant's risk of exposure.
    c) PPE available in the facility.
    d) client's physical appearance.

10. The nursing assistant should wear gloves when

    a) feeding a client in a common dining room.
    b) carrying linens from the linen closet to a client's room.
    c) leaving a client's room.
    d) washing a client's face and hands.

11. Thomas is taking care of an older client who has been placed on droplet precautions due to an upper respiratory infection. Thomas is assigned the client's morning bed bath. Before entering the client's room, Thomas puts on a(n)

    a) N95 respirator.
    b) isolation gown, gloves, and goggles.
    c) surgical mask.
    d) gown and gloves.

12. An example of a staph infection that is resistant to a number of antibiotics is

    a) TB.
    b) MRSA.
    c) *C. Diff.*
    d) VRE.

13. VRE infections occur most often in

    a) hospitals.
    b) the community.
    c) long-term care facilities.
    d) the client's home.

14. Employers often have nitrile and vinyl gloves available because

    a) most clients have latex allergies.
    b) OSHA requires employers to have a latex-free environment.
    c) many healthcare workers are allergic to latex.
    d) latex gloves do not protect the worker from pathogens.

7.E Choose the best response to the following scenarios.

1. You notice a coworker not washing hands in between caring for clients. What should you do?

    a) Mind your own business.
    b) Remind them of the importance of hand hygiene.
    c) Report them to your supervisor.
    d) Ask not to work with them.

2. Your client is upset and feels they are contaminated because everyone is wearing PPE when entering their room. What is your best response?

    a) Reassure them that the PPE is required to prevent the infection from spreading to others.
    b) Agree with them and tell them that you will take it off when no one else is looking.
    c) Tell the nurse to take them off precautions—it is just upsetting the client.
    d) Ask to be reassigned because the client is too emotionally exhausting.

3. Your client has been admitted to the hospital a third time with an infection obtained during a previous hospital stay. The client tells you it is the doctor's fault. What is the best response?

    a) Agree with the client—you know the doctor has bad infection rates.
    b) Listen sympathetically and assure the client you are there to help.
    c) Report the doctor to the charge nurse.
    d) Say nothing—the client does not understand how hospitals work.

4. Your employer offers you the flu vaccine, but you're unsure if you want the vaccination. What should you do?

    a) Try to avoid the situation as long as possible.
    b) Tell everyone how the employer is forcing you to become vaccinated.
    c) If indicated, receive the vaccination to help protect you and your clients from illness.
    d) Look for another job that doesn't require a flu shot.

5. You witness a coworker not wearing the proper PPE as indicated. When you remind your coworker of this, they say, "I'm not worried about it. It takes too long to put on." What is your best response?

    a) Agree with them; it is a time-consuming step.
    b) Remind them that the extra time to put on the PPE is protecting themselves and the client.
    c) Submit a complaint to the company newsletter.
    d) Tell your coworkers what you have just witnessed.

6. You are in a hurry and forget to wash your hands after leaving a client's room. What should you do?

    a) Remember to hand sanitize next time.
    b) Do nothing and go to the next client.
    c) Rub your hands on your uniform.
    d) Use your hand sanitizer before touching anything else.

Name _____

Chapter 8: Body Mechanics and Workplace Safety

8.A Matching Definitions

_____ 1. Employee assistance plan (EAP)
_____ 2. Pivot Disc
_____ 3. Safety Data Sheets (SDSs)
_____ 4. RACE
_____ 5. Ergonomics
_____ 6. PASS

A. Acronym used to remember how to use the fire extinguisher: Pull, Aim, Squeeze, and Sweep

B. An agreement between the employer and an insurance company and/or mental health provider to provide employees with free services for workers and their families

C. OSHA-mandated sheets that give detailed information about what each chemical is and what first aid to use if an exposure occurs

D. Adapting work style and environment to increase safety and minimize discomfort

E. Acronym used to remember how to respond to a fire: Resident or Rescue, Alarm or Activate Alarm, Confine, and Extinguish or Evacuate

F. An assistive device used in transferring a client who can bear weight but who may not have the ability to take steps or move sideways easily

8.B Reflective Short-Answer Exercises

Chrystal works as a nursing assistant at a local nursing home. They normally work the 3:00 p.m. to 11:00 p.m. shift. At times, it is hard to find a coworker to help them reposition and move clients. Today Chrystal was trying to move a client from their wheelchair to the toilet by themselves, even though the care plan indicates that they are a two-person assist. During the transfer, the client became unsteady and fell. Chrystal tried their best to prevent the fall, but in the process hurt their back. The client is now complaining of knee pain.

1. What factors led to the fall and resulting injuries?

_____
_____
_____
_____

2. What steps could Chrystal have taken to prevent the injuries from happening?

_____
_____
_____
_____

Name _____

3. What lifestyle choices can Chrystal make to prevent further injuries to themselves?

_____
_____
_____
_____

4. Will Chrystal get in trouble for this event? Why or why not?

_____
_____
_____
_____

5. To whom must Chrystal report this accident?

_____
_____
_____
_____

6. What documentation must be completed after this event?

_____
_____
_____
_____

8.C Fill in the blanks using terms found in the word bank.

employer	walkways	hide
RACE	blood-borne pathogens	insurance company
OSHA	physically	dangerous
PASS	fight	emergency plans
chemical	emergency codes	ergonomics
run	workplace violence	

1. An agreement between the _____ and a(n) _____. It provides employees with free mental healthcare services for themselves or a family member via the employee assistance program (EAP).

2. _____ is adapting work style and the work environment to be safer.

3. _____ is much more common in healthcare than in other types of employment.

4. _____ can be found in body fluids other than blood, such as vomit, saliva, wound drainage, urine, feces, semen, vaginal secretions, and wound drainage.

5. _____ is the acronym used for Rescue, Alarm, Contain, and Extinguish.

6. Employers are a mandated by _____ to offer the hepatitis B vaccine series to all workers who may be exposed to blood-borne pathogens.

38 • Chapter 8

Name _____

7. _____ is the acronym used to remember how to use the fire extinguisher.

8. Working in healthcare can be _____ if you do not follow OSHA (Occupational Safety and Health Administration) and employer policies.

9. A nursing assistant has a very _____ demanding job. It is necessary to stay in good shape.

10. _____ are used to quickly convey emergency information to facility employees.

11. Make sure _____ and client rooms are free of any obstacles on the floor.

12. Safety Data Sheets (SDSs) give detailed information about what each _____ is and suggest what first aid to use if an exposure occurs.

13. Every healthcare facility must have _____ in place in the event of a natural disaster.

14. To keep yourself and others safe during an active shooter attack you will need to choose to _____, _____, or _____ depending on your unique situation.

8.D Multiple-Choice Exercises

1. Healthcare workers are at risk of exposure to blood-borne pathogens present in
    a) urine and feces.
    b) wound drainage.
    c) vomit and saliva.
    d) all of the above.

2. Information found in the SDS includes
    a) the client's diagnosis and care plan.
    b) how to store or dispose of chemicals.
    c) ergonomic recommendations.
    d) fire safety plans.

3. Stephan's care plan states that they are to be transferred with an assist of one. This morning when you try to assist Stephan, they are very weak and shaky. You should
    a) have them remain in bed.
    b) find a coworker to assist you.
    c) tell the nurse to change their care plan.
    d) have another nurse assistant toilet them for you.

4. You have just entered the dining area, when you notice smoke coming from the kitchen. Your FIRST response is to
    a) call the fire department.
    b) pull the fire alarm.
    c) grab the fire extinguisher.
    d) place clients beyond the fire doors.

5. Healthcare workers can reduce the risk of injury by lifting with
    a) their backs.
    b) the object away from the body.
    c) the hip and thigh muscles.
    d) their feet close together.

6. When using a fire extinguisher, you should
    a) aim and sweep along the base of the fire.
    b) aim the extinguisher at the base and hold still.
    c) aim and sweep at the fire's flames.
    d) aim at the flames and hold still.

7. Nursing assistants are trained on a facility's emergency plans
    a) at their 3-month review.
    b) at their time of hire.
    c) only if they work the evening shift.
    d) only if they work in acute care.

8. In the case of an evacuation, the nursing assistant may have to
    a) go with the clients during transportation to a new area.
    b) take on laundry and kitchen duties.
    c) care for more clients than usual.
    d) do all of the above.

Name _____

9. An employee assistance plan (EAP) is an agreement that provides

   a) free services to employees only.
   b) free services to employees and their families.
   c) health benefits to employers.
   d) health information to employers.

10. The MOST important step in protecting yourself from workplace violence is to

    a) keep doors locked at all times.
    b) work only with people you know and trust.
    c) watch for potentially dangerous situations.
    d) work during the day shift.

8.E Choose the best response to the following scenarios.

1. While plugging in a client's television, you notice a spark and smoke. What should you do?

   a) Wait and make sure the television works well.
   b) Tell the client to get it fixed soon.
   c) Unplug the television and report to the supervisor immediately.
   d) Bring in your television for the client.

2. While at work in the nursing home, you notice your hands start to itch; by the end of the day, you have a rash on your hands. What should you do?

   a) Wash your hands and report to your supervisor immediately.
   b) Use hand sanitizer instead of soap and water.
   c) Wear gloves to further eliminate any exposure.
   d) Wait until the next day to update your supervisor.

3. Your client's care plan indicates that you use a mechanical lift to transfer them to the wheelchair. Your coworker requests that you try to stand the client with their assistance. What should you do?

   a) Stand the client for the transfer.
   b) Ask the client how they want to transfer.
   c) Follow the care plan.
   d) Report your coworker to your supervisor.

4. You are working as a nursing assistant in the nursing home, and you have a fire drill the same time that you are scheduled to take your break. What should you do?

   a) Take your break anyway.
   b) Ask your coworkers what they would do.
   c) Request that the drill time be changed.
   d) Report to your supervisor for instruction.

5. You answer the phone while working at the hospital, and Channel 9 News asks you about the bomb threat that happened yesterday. What should you do?

   a) Explain the situation in detail to decrease rumors.
   b) Place them on hold and get your supervisor to take the call.
   c) Give the information only if you are compensated.
   d) Give the phone to another nurse assistant who has more experience.

6. A coworker constantly belittles you in front of clients and other employees. What should you do?

   a) Politely but firmly ask the coworker to stop the behavior.
   b) Get the other employees to pick on them.
   c) Avoid the coworker as much as you can.
   d) Find another job so you don't have to work with them.

Name _____

Chapter 9: Reducing Client Injury and Falls

9.A Matching Definitions

_____ 1. Ambulatory

_____ 2. Gait

_____ 3. Orthostatic hypotension

A. Rapid drop in blood pressure that occurs when moving from a lying to sitting position, or from sitting to standing position

B. Having the ability to walk about

C. A pattern of walking

9.B Reflective Short-Answer Exercises

Sally is an 84-year-old who lives at home. Sally is the primary caregiver for their partner Chris, who has dementia. One night while going to the bathroom, Sally tripped on a throw rug and fell. Sally was unable to get up on their own, and Chris could not assist Sally. Sally lay on the floor until their daughter came to visit the next day. Sally's fall resulted in a broken hip and arm. After staying in the hospital for 3 nights, Sally is transferred to a nursing home for rehabilitation services.

1. What do you think will happen to Sally's partner while they are recovering from their fall?

   _____
   _____
   _____
   _____

2. What emotions do you think Sally will experience while in the hospital and nursing home?

   _____
   _____
   _____
   _____

3. What steps can the nursing assistant take to help Sally while they are in the hospital and nursing home?

   _____
   _____
   _____
   _____

4. What factors do you think could have contributed to Sally's fall?

   _____
   _____
   _____
   _____

5. What steps could have been taken to prevent Sally from falling?

   _____
   _____
   _____
   _____

Name _____

9.C Fill in the blanks using terms found in the word bank.

ambulatory	alarm systems	nursing assistant
upright	programs	fall
strengthening	gait	death rates
EMS		

1. If a client has the ability to walk, this is referred to as being _____.
2. _____ is the person's pattern of walking.
3. Most injuries that occur to people over the age of 65 result from a _____.
4. _____ from falls have risen over the last decade.
5. The _____ must be in tune with the client at all times.
6. Never hold a client _____ during a fall; you can injure yourself and the client.
7. The nursing assistant may need to help _____ move a client who was seriously injured onto a stretcher.
8. There are many different _____ and initiatives to help prevent falls.
9. Balance retraining and _____ exercises can help reduce the risk of falls.
10. Some facilities use _____ for clients who are at risk of falling.

9.D Multiple-Choice Exercises

1. A fall in an older client may lead to
   a) increase in level of care.
   b) immobility.
   c) depression.
   d) all of the above.

2. Grace is an older client of yours who has had two recent falls. You notice that you have to tell Grace to look up when they are walking. Grace looks down at their feet instead. This is likely because Grace is
   a) not listening to you.
   b) afraid of falling again.
   c) not able to follow directions.
   d) not steady enough to walk.

3. All of the following put a client at risk of falling EXCEPT
   a) buildup of earwax.
   b) frequent naps.
   c) antidepressant medications.
   d) walking without shoes.

4. You are ambulating a client using a gait belt and a walker. The client suddenly becomes weak and begins to fall. You should
   a) try to catch them before they fall to the floor.
   b) have them lean on the walker until they are rested and steady.
   c) lower them to the floor using the gait belt and both hands.
   d) lower them to the floor with one hand on the gait belt.

5. After a witnessed fall, the nurse is likely to ask that vital signs be taken
   a) once each shift for the next 24 hours.
   b) once each shift for the next week.
   c) at the time of the fall only.
   d) once each shift for the next 72 hours.

Name _____

6. David has fallen in their room. The nurse directs you to assist David to their bed, but they are too weak to help with the transfer. You should

   a) use a gait belt and an assist of two to help them to their feet.
   b) put a sheet under them and ask a coworker to help lift them.
   c) use a mechanical lift to move them to their bed.
   d) allow them to rest and to regain their strength before moving them.

7. The FIRST step in preventing falls is

   a) assisting clients with their basic needs.
   b) providing exercise classes.
   c) placing alarms on wheelchairs and beds as needed.
   d) identifying who is at risk of a fall.

8. One example of a fall prevention strategy would be

   a) encouraging a client to attend activities.
   b) having a client lie in bed as much as possible.
   c) lowering a client to the floor if they become weak.
   d) placing a pressure alarm on a client's wheelchair.

9. Elena often gets out of bed to walk to the bathroom. Yesterday Elena tripped on their bedside table and fell. An appropriate fall prevention strategy would be to

   a) place a soft mat on the floor next to their bed.
   b) have them go to bed earlier so they are more alert.
   c) post a sign reminding them to ask for help.
   d) place a tab alarm on their bed.

10. The person MOST at risk of falling would be a

    a) 30-year-old who had gallbladder surgery.
    b) 77-year-old living at home and on pain medications.
    c) 21-year-old who takes medication for depression.
    d) 67-year-old with a history of asthma.

11. Dennis is an older client at risk of falling because they forget to lock their wheelchair brakes before standing. The BEST way to prevent Dennis from falling is to

    a) tell them that they are not allowed to stand by themself.
    b) place them by the nurse's desk with the wheels locked.
    c) put leg rests on the wheelchair to keep them from standing.
    d) have anti-roll-back brakes placed on their wheelchair.

9.E Choose the best response to the following scenarios.

1. Your client is placed on bed rest following surgery but insists they can walk to the bathroom with your assistance. What should you do?

   a) Help the client to the restroom; it is best to keep them moving.
   b) Get another nursing assistant to assist you in case they are not strong enough.
   c) Reinforce to the client the importance of remaining on bed rest and offer the bedpan.
   d) Ask the nurse to assist the client to the bathroom.

2. Your home care client is at risk for falls due to several throw rugs in their path. What should you do?

   a) Remove the rugs and place them in a closet.
   b) Remind the client that the rugs pose a danger and then report to your supervisor.
   c) Buy rugs with nonskid grip for the client.
   d) Call the client's daughter and ask them to remove the rugs.

Name _____

3. While ambulating a client, they state that they are dizzy. What should you do?

   a) Assist the client to a sitting position.
   b) Keep going until the dizziness passes.
   c) Allow them to stand and regain their strength.
   d) Tighten your grip on the transfer belt in case they fall.

4. You witness a client fall in their bedroom. What should you do?

   a) Help the client back to their feet.
   b) Go looking for another nursing assistant to help you.
   c) Help the client into bed and then alert the nurse.
   d) Stay with the client and yell for the nurse.

5. Your client continuously uses the call light system and does not need immediate assistance. What should you do?

   a) Take the call light away.
   b) Hide the call light.
   c) Continue to answer the call light.
   d) Only answer the call light every half hour.

6. You notice one of your clients with dementia crawling around on the floor of their room. What should you do?

   a) Ask the nurse to sedate the client with medication.
   b) Nicely ask the client to stop being so disruptive.
   c) Put the client back in bed and tell them to remain there.
   d) Make sure the client is safe and try to redirect them.

Name _____

Chapter 10: Restraints and Restraint Alternatives

10.A Definitions

In your own words, write a definition of the following term.

1. Restraint: _____

10.B Reflective Short-Answer Exercises

Gerry suffers from dementia. When you take them to the bathroom or attempt to bathe them, they become very aggressive. Gerry spits, pinches, and shouts obscenities. Tonight, when you were getting them ready for bed, they punched you in the face, causing a black eye.

1. Will restraining Gerry decrease their aggressive behaviors? Why or why not?

2. What risks are there for Gerry if they are restrained?

3. Do you think giving Gerry a medication for their aggression might help? Why or why not?

4. What are the risks of starting an anti-anxiety or antipsychotic medication?

5. What are some alternative ways you could reduce Gerry's aggressive behavior instead of restraining them?

Name _____

10.C Fill in the blanks using terms found in the word bank.

Two	physical	restraint
range-of-motion	Medicare	safety
2 hours	Medicaid	emotional
bed frame	safety	15 minutes
chemical		

1. A _____ is any physical or chemical limitation that prevents movement.
2. The Centers for _____ & _____ Services have rules to make sure that clients can freely move about their environment.
3. The _____ main categories of restraints are physical and chemical.
4. The goal of restraining is to protect the _____ of the client or those around them.
5. The use of restraints can increase the risk of _____ and _____ harm.
6. If a restraint is used, the client must be checked every _____.
7. Every _____, the restraint must be removed.
8. Perform _____ exercises on the bed-bound client when the restraint is removed.
9. A restraint must be secured to the _____.
10. The only appropriate reason to use a restraint is to ensure _____.
11. A _____ restraint is an anti-anxiety or antipsychotic drug.

10.D Multiple-Choice Exercises

1. The use of restraints can
    a) keep a client safe from falls.
    b) prevent physical outbursts.
    c) decrease aggressive behavior.
    d) cause depression.

2. A restraint may be used for a client if
    a) the facility doesn't have enough staff.
    b) the client has been hitting staff and yelling at others.
    c) it is needed to treat the client's medical condition.
    d) the client has a history of falls.

3. One of your clients has a wrist restraint. You should check the hand, fingers, and the area under the restraint every
    a) 2 hours.
    b) 15 minutes.
    c) hour.
    d) 30 minutes.

4. Joe has restraints on their ankles. You should alert the nurse right away if
    a) Joe's foot feels warm when you touch it.
    b) Joe complains that their foot feels numb.
    c) Joe does foot exercises on their own.
    d) Joe needs their incontinence product changed.

5. One of your clients has a wrist restraint. You will need to check their
    a) legs every 15 minutes.
    b) arms and hands every 30 minutes.
    c) arms and hands every 15 minutes.
    d) legs and feet every 20 minutes.

6. A nursing assistant may apply a restraint if
    a) a client is at risk of falling out of bed.
    b) the nurse decides it is necessary.
    c) it is ordered by the client's doctor.
    d) it stops the client from wandering outside.

7. Elsa is an older client who has a lot of anxiety and becomes easily upset. The doctor orders medication to help with their anxiety. Today Elsa had to be assisted with their lunch because they were very drowsy. This is an example of a(n)

   a) chemical restraint.
   b) environmental restraint.
   c) normal part of aging.
   d) negligence.

8. Wilson recently had surgery on their hip. Wilson has asked you to put their side rails up to make it easier for them to move in bed. You should

   a) put the side rails up, since they are using them for positioning.
   b) tell them that side rails are a restraint and shouldn't be used.
   c) put the side rails up after the nurse gets informed consent.
   d) instruct the client on side rail risks and then put them up.

9. A nursing assistant can help prevent the use of restraints by

   a) placing an alarm on clients' wheelchairs.
   b) keeping clients on routine schedules.
   c) telling clients' families they need to visit daily.
   d) using side rails to keep clients in bed.

10. Some facilities have taken side rails off all of the clients' beds because

    a) clients may get their arms or legs caught.
    b) clients are at risk of strangling themselves.
    c) positioning devices are available and are not restraints.
    d) all of the above.

11. Carlos has wrist restraints applied due to agitation and risk of hurting themself. The use of the restraints may lead to any of the following EXCEPT

    a) pressure injuries.
    b) decreased agitation.
    c) emotional upset.
    d) muscle weakness.

12. Before side rails may be applied, the nurse needs to get

    a) an order from the doctor only.
    b) verbal consent from the client's family.
    c) a signed waiver from the client or their power of attorney.
    d) a doctor's order and a signed waiver.

10.E Choose the best response to the following scenarios.

1. Your client asks you to raise the side rail of the bed before leaving the room. What should you do?

   a) Raise the side rail for them—it is their right.
   b) Refuse to raise the rail and tell them that it is not safe.
   c) Raise both rails and make sure the bed is in the low position.
   d) Tell your supervisor that they are asking for side rails.

2. The nurse in acute care has obtained a doctor's order for soft wrist restraints and asks you to apply them to a confused client. What is your best response?

   a) Place the wrist restraints on the client as directed.
   b) Tell the nurse that soft wrist restraints cannot be used in the acute care setting.
   c) Tell the nurse that they will need to apply the restraint and then you can assist afterward.
   d) Tell the nurse that you feel a chemical restraint would be more appropriate.

Name _____

3. Your client continues to unfasten their waist restraint and stand up. What should you do?

   a) Tie it in a knot.
   b) Place it behind the chair.
   c) Take it off.
   d) Update the supervisor.

4. An older, confused client is yelling and disrupting the other clients in the dining area. What should you do?

   a) Take them to their room and shut the door.
   b) Try to anticipate what they may need.
   c) Tell them to sit down and be respectful of others.
   d) Move all of the residents away from them.

5. You have completed your shift for the day. On the way home, you remember that a side rail on one of your clients' beds has been left up. What should you do?

   a) Forget about it.
   b) Drive back and lower it.
   c) Lower it tomorrow.
   d) Call the facility and report.

6. Your client continues to wander into other clients' rooms with their wheelchair. What should you do?

   a) Lock their wheelchair so that they cannot roam.
   b) Put them in a recliner with the legs up.
   c) Invite them to go for a walk with you.
   d) Put them in front of the television.

Chapter 11: Basic First Aid Measures

11.A Matching Definitions

_____ 1. Complete airway obstruction

_____ 2. Full-thickness burn

_____ 3. Hypovolemic shock

_____ 4. Status epilepticus

_____ 5. Cardiogenic shock

_____ 6. Partial-thickness burn

_____ 7. Partial airway obstruction

_____ 8. Cardiac arrest

_____ 9. Syncope

_____ 10. Dangling

_____ 11. Aura

_____ 12. Seizure

_____ 13. Hemorrhage

_____ 14. Anaphylactic shock

_____ 15. Superficial burn

A. Uncontrollable dilation of all the blood vessels, usually from an allergic reaction

B. Disrupted electrical activity within the brain

C. The heart cannot effectively pump blood; may be caused by a heart attack

D. The heart cannot contract and pump blood; usually a result of heart attack or trauma

E. Sitting on the side of the bed after moving from a lying position; allows time for blood pressure to stabilize

F. Type of burn that involves the epidermis, dermis, and subcutaneous tissue; may also affect deep muscles and tendons

G. Excessive loss of blood, either internal or external

H. A feeling or a visual disturbance experienced prior to a seizure

I. Type of burn that involves the epidermis and dermis

J. Fainting; a sudden, temporary loss of consciousness

K. Blood and fluid loss so extreme that the heart is unable to pump enough blood to support the body

L. Blockage of the airway that still allows for some air exchange

M. Very little to no air exchange due to blockage of the airway

N. A life-threatening generalized seizure that lasts longer than 5 minutes

O. Type of burn that involves only the top layer of skin, the epidermis

Name _____

11.B Reflective Short-Answer Exercises

You are working in an assisted-living facility. Damon, one of your clients, starts coughing violently. Damon stands up and starts walking to their room. By the time they get to their room, you hear their cough getting weaker. As you approach, they shake their head no, indicating that they do not want your help. You notice that they have now turned red and have a high-pitched wheeze.

1. Why would Damon walk away during a potentially life-threatening situation?

   _____
   _____
   _____
   _____

2. Should you give them their privacy? Why or why not?

   _____
   _____
   _____
   _____

3. Should you attempt to start abdominal thrusts? Why or why not?

   _____
   _____
   _____
   _____

4. Did Damon originally have a partial or complete obstruction?

   _____
   _____
   _____
   _____

5. What are the symptoms of a partial obstruction?

   _____
   _____
   _____
   _____

6. What type of foreign body airway obstruction did they ultimately have?

   _____
   _____
   _____
   _____

Name _____

7. What are the symptoms of a complete obstruction?
_____
_____
_____
_____

8. When should you have activated EMS?
_____
_____
_____
_____

11.C Fill in the blanks using terms found in the word bank.

epidermis   seizure   FBAO
consciousness   anaphylactic shock   brain
cardiac arrest   sitting   cardiogenic shock
complete airway obstruction   emergencies   life-threatening
blood

1. _____ is a severe reaction that causes uncontrolled dilation of all the blood vessels in the body.

2. A full-thickness burn is a type of burn that involves the _____, dermis, and subcutaneous tissue.

3. _____ is the ineffective contraction of the heart causing severely impaired circulation of blood. One possible cause is a heart attack.

4. An aura is a feeling or a visual disturbance experienced prior to a _____.

5. _____ is when the heart does not pump enough blood to the organs of the body due to severe damage to the heart.

6. A(n) _____ means there is little to no air exchange.

7. Dangling is _____ on the side of the bed to allow time for the blood pressure to stabilize.

8. Hypovolemic shock can result from an extreme loss of _____.

9. A seizure is caused by disrupted electrical activity within the _____.

10. Status epilepticus is a(n) _____ generalized seizure that lasts longer than 5 minutes.

11. Syncope is a sudden, temporary loss of _____ usually due to a decreased oxygen level in the brain.

12. _____ will arise. You will need to be ready for them.

13. A(n) _____ is a blockage of the throat that results in choking.

Chapter 11 • 51

Name _____

11.D Multiple-Choice Exercises

1. You are assisting clients with their lunch when you notice that one of the clients takes a large bite of potatoes. They start coughing. You should

   a) ask them if they are choking and then do abdominal thrusts.
   b) have them take a drink of water.
   c) remain close and allow them to cough.
   d) ask them to raise their arms into the air.

2. High-pitched wheezing is a symptom of a

   a) complete airway obstruction.
   b) syncopal episode.
   c) partial airway obstruction.
   d) grand mal seizure.

3. A leading cause of cardiac arrest is

   a) status epilepticus.
   b) extreme blood loss.
   c) chronic obstructive pulmonary disease.
   d) spinal cord injury.

4. Once cardiopulmonary resuscitation (CPR) is started, it can only be stopped if

   a) you are no longer able to feel a pulse.
   b) the ambulance driver declares the client dead.
   c) someone qualified takes over.
   d) it has been longer than 6 minutes since it was started.

5. You are walking with Alma using a gait belt and pulling a wheelchair behind them. Alma suddenly becomes shaky and weak. Alma says that they see "dark spots." The FIRST thing you should do is

   a) get them some water or juice to drink.
   b) have them sit down in the wheelchair.
   c) report their symptoms to the nurse.
   d) take them outside for fresh air.

6. "Dangling" means that before assisting a client to stand, you

   a) allow time for the blood pressure to stabilize.
   b) make sure that the client's feet are flat on the floor.
   c) make sure that the client has their shoes and socks on.
   d) allow the client's feet to swing freely while sitting.

7. A client experiencing a generalized seizure

   a) has a weak pulse and low blood pressure.
   b) has chest pain and grayish skin.
   c) looks like they are staring off into space.
   d) collapses and shakes uncontrollably.

8. When a client is having a seizure, the nursing assistant should

   a) hold the client in place so they don't hit anything.
   b) place a spoon in their mouth to prevent swallowing the tongue.
   c) note what time the seizure starts and ends.
   d) activate EMS if the seizure lasts longer than 5 minutes.

9. You enter a client's room to find them lying on the floor. They are bleeding from a large cut across their forehead. The FIRST thing you should do is

   a) put on a pair of gloves.
   b) activate your EMS.
   c) apply sterile dressings to the forehead.
   d) assist them to a recovery position.

Name _____

10. Doris is an older client who has fallen and has a gash across their left arm. You apply pressure to the wound using a sterile dressing. The dressing is soaked through, and the bleeding is not slowing. Your next step should be to

   a) remove the soaked dressing before applying a new dressing to the wound.
   b) apply another dressing on top of the soiled dressing and pressure to the artery above the wound.
   c) apply a tourniquet above the gash to stop the bleeding from the wound.
   d) place them in the recovery position and elevate their legs to increase circulation to the heart.

11. The type of shock caused by extreme blood loss is called

   a) hypovolemic.
   b) syncopal.
   c) cardiogenic.
   d) anaphylactic.

12. Symptoms of shock include all of the following EXCEPT

   a) cool and clammy skin.
   b) a weak pulse.
   c) decreased respiratory rate.
   d) a drop in blood pressure.

13. A partial-thickness burn is

   a) red, sensitive, and involves the epidermis only.
   b) painful and involves the muscles and tendons.
   c) not painful because of nerve damage.
   d) painful, swollen, and blistered.

14. You are assisting a client who has burned themself. After you activate the EMS, your NEXT step is to

   a) cover the burn with a cool, damp cloth.
   b) cover the burn with a dry sterile dressing.
   c) put a burn ointment on the wound.
   d) take vital signs and document the incident.

15. Carlos is an older adult client with dementia. You discover them in the housekeeping closet and notice that they have redness around their mouth. The FIRST step you should take is to

   a) find out what they ate or drank.
   b) activate the EMS.
   c) contact the poison center.
   d) rinse their mouth with water.

16. A client has accidentally spilled bathroom cleaner on their skin. To find information about this chemical, a nursing assistant should

   a) contact the emergency room.
   b) call the client's doctor.
   c) look up the chemical in the SDS.
   d) look it up on Wikipedia.

11.E Choose the best response to the following scenarios.

1. One of your clients is coughing and obviously choking. What should you do?

   a) Start chest compressions.
   b) Call 911.
   c) Stand by and wait to help if needed.
   d) Offer a drink of water.

2. You find your client on the floor with no pulse. The client has expressed in the past that they do not want to be resuscitated. What should you do?

   a) Yell for help and start CPR.
   b) Activate EMS.
   c) Put the call light on.
   d) Call the client's doctor.

Name _____

3. You are ambulating your client, and they have a syncopal episode. What should you do?

   a) Put them in the recliner with their feet elevated.
   b) Help them to the floor while protecting their head.
   c) Take them to the restroom after the episode.
   d) Give them a drink of water and cool them off.

4. You are sitting at the breakfast table with a client who has a seizure. What should you do?

   a) Clear the room.
   b) Send your coworker for an ice pack.
   c) Note the time and keep the client safe.
   d) Do all of the above.

5. One of your clients may have ingested some household cleaner. What should you do?

   a) Report to the supervisor immediately.
   b) Give them a glass of milk.
   c) Make them vomit.
   d) Wait and see what happens.

6. One of your clients dies from an internal hemorrhage. The client's daughter tells you it was because the EMS service was too slow. What is the best response?

   a) Inform the daughter that the death had nothing to do with the EMS service's response time.
   b) Give the daughter the name of a well-known lawyer.
   c) Agree with the daughter but tell them that you can't comment.
   d) Express sympathy and report this comment to your supervisor.

Name _____

Chapter 12: Holistic Care of Clients

12.A Matching Definitions

_____ 1. Quality of life

_____ 2. Nonpharmacological pain management

_____ 3. Holistic care

_____ 4. Esteem

_____ 5. Self-actualization

_____ 6. Homeostasis

A. Admiration or respect

B. State in which internal body processes remain stable despite outside variables

C. Meeting one's own emotional, social, creative, and spiritual needs

D. A measure of happiness in regard to emotional health, physical comfort, spiritual wellness, and social activity

E. Paying attention to and caring for a client's emotional, physical, social, and spiritual needs

F. Managing pain without the use of drugs

12.B Reflective Short-Answer Exercises

You are working in a long-term care facility. You care for Gene, who has dementia and does not talk to the staff or the other clients. Gene is sitting next to the nurse's station, waiting for their partner to come. You notice that they look upset. When you ask Gene if something is wrong, they just shake their head and look away from you.

1. List some examples of how you might be able to help Gene meet each of Maslow's hierarchy of needs.

_____
_____
_____
_____

2. What developmental stage do you think Gene might be in? Why?

_____
_____
_____
_____

3. What could be wrong with Gene?

_____
_____
_____
_____

4. What should you do to help them?

5. How do you know if your interventions worked or not? What signs would you see?

6. How could you positively affect Gene's quality of life?

7. How can you care for this client holistically? List specific interventions that can help them meet their emotional, physical, and spiritual needs.

8. What kind of social activities could Gene participate in if they are not verbal?

9. How could you meet the needs of Gene's partner when they visit?

12.C Fill in the blanks using terms found in the word bank.

milestones	physical	Abraham Maslow
pain	emotional	religious beliefs
enhances	measure	nonverbal
quality of life	internal	

Name _____

1. Giving holistic care means the nursing assistant is caring for the _____, _____, and spiritual needs of the client.
2. Homeostasis is the state in which _____ body processes remain stable.
3. _____ is a measure of happiness in regard to emotional health, physical comfort, spiritual wellness, and social activity.
4. Human beings have basic needs. _____ was a psychologist who studied people and their needs.
5. Normal human development is measured based on when a person achieves certain _____ at a given point in their life.
6. Tending to the comfort of your client _____ their quality of life.
7. Physical comfort is another _____ of quality of life.
8. Having _____ can severely diminish a person's quality of life.
9. _____ clients express their discomfort in various ways other than telling you.
10. You must never force your own _____ upon the client.

12.D Multiple-Choice Exercises

1. Providing holistic care means paying attention to
   a) the client's physical and emotional needs.
   b) the client's social and spiritual needs.
   c) the client's illness and level of function.
   d) both a and b.

2. Joanne is working in their garden. It is nearly 90 degrees and they are sweating. This is an example of
   a) homeostasis.
   b) adaptation.
   c) elimination.
   d) physical comfort.

3. The social, creative, emotional, and spiritual potential in a person is called
   a) self-realization.
   b) self-image.
   c) self-actualization.
   d) self-image.

4. Luther has worked at a local factory for the last several years but has lost their job. They are having a difficult time supporting their family and themself. According to Maslow, the level of need Luther will meet when they find new employment is
   a) esteem.
   b) safety.
   c) love and belonging.
   d) basic human needs.

5. Encouraging client participation in a tour of a local art exhibit helps the client to meet their need for
   a) esteem.
   b) love and belonging.
   c) comfort.
   d) self-actualization.

6. The typical age when a child develops a sense of identity through experimentation is
   a) 2–3 years old.
   b) 4–5 years old.
   c) 6–11 years old.
   d) 12–19 years old.

Name _____

7. Self-confidence and cooperation with others develops when a person is

   a) 4–5 years old.
   b) 6–11 years old.
   c) 12–19 years old.
   d) 20–34 years old.

8. The FIRST step in helping a client who is emotionally unwell is to

   a) ensure that they are toileted promptly.
   b) offer them a chance to paint or put together puzzles.
   c) make sure that they don't wander into unsafe areas.
   d) encourage them to participate in activities.

9. You are taking care of Molly and notice that their chart states that they are Catholic. Molly is resting but you realize that your facility has Catholic services being held in the chapel. You should

   a) get Molly ready for church.
   b) let Molly continue resting.
   c) ask Molly if they would like to attend church.
   d) wait and take Molly to the next service.

10. John's partner comes in to visit them almost daily. The partner always seems upset and tearful when they leave. Today you have an opportunity to sit and get to know them better. This can

    a) improve customer satisfaction.
    b) decrease their stress.
    c) increase their quality of life.
    d) do all of the above.

11. The FIRST step in helping a client with relaxation breathing is to:

    a) have them take a deep breath through the mouth.
    b) ask the client to place their hands on their abdomen.
    c) ask the client to take a deep breath in through the nose.
    d) have them think of a soothing memory.

12.E Choose the best response to the following scenarios.

1. Your client can button their shirt, but it takes them a long time. You have a lot of work to get done in a short amount of time. What should you do?

   a) Button the shirt for them.
   b) Let the client button their shirt.
   c) Buy them pullover shirts.
   d) Tell them to hurry.

2. A coworker has told your client that if they do not take a bath today, they will not allow the client to attend church tonight. What should you do?

   a) Report this to your supervisor.
   b) Reinforce this with the client.
   c) Tell your coworker not to say such things.
   d) Apologize to the client on your coworker's behalf.

3. To maintain independence, your client eats with their fingers. What should you do?

   a) Place the different foods in small bowls.
   b) Feed them so that they don't get messy.
   c) Provide them with finger foods.
   d) Ask that they eat in their room.

4. Your client stays in their room most of the time and will not talk to anyone but their wife. What should you do?

   a) Offer activities but respect their privacy.
   b) Take them to bingo per their wife's request.
   c) Limit your contact with them.
   d) Trade assignments with a coworker.

Name _____

5. Your client's husband died a year ago. Since then, they go through periods of depression. What should you do?

   a) Encourage them to develop a relationship with another client who is interested in them.
   b) Actively listen when they talk about their husband and ask questions about their life together.
   c) Ignore the behavior when they get into one of these moods.
   d) Call their daughter to tell them they need to come and visit their mother.

6. You have an older client who is in pain. They cannot have their prescription pain medication at this time. What should you do?

   a) Explain to them that they must wait 2 more hours before receiving more pain medication.
   b) Turn down the lights and reposition them.
   c) Give them an ice pack to put on the painful area.
   d) Ask their family to bring in some Tylenol® for them.

This page intentionally left blank.

Name _____

Chapter 13: Client Room Environment

13.A Matching Definitions

No definitions listed in the textbook.

13.B Reflective Short-Answer Exercises

Herman is an older client with dementia. Herman is no longer safe to stay at home alone because they have been wandering out of their home and getting lost. Home health care is not an option since they need 24-hour supervision. Herman's daughter is trying to decide if they need to go to an assisted-living facility or long-term care facility.

1. What basic human needs must the facility meet to care for Herman?

   _____
   _____
   _____
   _____

2. What should Herman's daughter be looking for when touring the individual rooms at each facility?

   _____
   _____
   _____
   _____

3. Are there certain indicators of cleanliness and safety that the daughter should be looking for while touring the facilities?

   _____
   _____
   _____
   _____

4. What factors would indicate poor quality of care?

   _____
   _____
   _____

5. What should each facility look like?

   _____
   _____
   _____
   _____

Name _____

6. What should each facility smell like?
   _____
   _____
   _____
   _____

7. What aspects of Herman's room can the family adapt to make their transition into a long-term care facility easier?
   _____
   _____
   _____
   _____

8. What aspects of Herman's room can the family adapt to make their transition into an assisted-living facility easier?
   _____
   _____
   _____
   _____

9. What considerations must the daughter keep in mind when making the decision between assisted living and long-term care?
   _____
   _____
   _____
   _____

13.C Fill in the blanks using terms found in the word bank.

privacy	safety	minimum
smelling	rights	call-light system
alarms	clients	assisted-living
bathroom	water	welcoming

1. In 1987, Congress mandated that residents in long-term care (LTC) facilities have certain _____.
2. The Omnibus Budget Reconciliation Act (OBRA) includes resident rights such as safety, respect, _____, and quality of life.
3. Long-term care facilities have become more _____ to the healthcare consumer.
4. _____ is a basic human right and need.
5. There must be a(n) _____ of one common room for dining and activities in each long-term care facility.
6. The long-term care facility must guarantee a safe _____ supply.

7. In older long-term care buildings, there may not be a(n) _____ within each client room, so clients might have to share.

8. A(n) _____ must be in place and operational to ensure the safety of long-term care residents.

9. _____ are tools occasionally used to alert staff that at-risk clients may be in danger.

10. Keeping the bathroom clean can prevent the facility from _____ unpleasant.

11. Long-term care facilities are renovating and decorating to attract new _____ that are now used to having many choices.

12. The atmosphere of new _____ facilities is warm and inviting to attract the new savvy healthcare consumer.

13.D Multiple-Choice Exercises

1. OBRA regulations apply to aspects of a client's room and environment in
   a) acute care facilities.
   b) assisted-living centers.
   c) skilled nursing facilities.
   d) respite care facilities.

2. A nursing home that does not have fire evacuation plans in place is likely to
   a) lose its license to provide care.
   b) be cited and pay penalties.
   c) be unable to accept new clients.
   d) close until plans are made.

3. If a nursing home has a dining room too small for its clients and their equipment, the facility should
   a) leave the equipment outside the dining room.
   b) have some clients eat in their rooms.
   c) set up tables in the hallway.
   d) rotate the client's meal times.

4. Long-term care facilities are required to have all of the following EXCEPT
   a) an air-conditioning system.
   b) hand rails on both sides of hallways.
   c) a fully equipped room for dining and activities.
   d) a safe water supply.

5. Sarah and their roommate have very different personalities and have not been getting along. Sarah is asking to move to a new room. You should
   a) move them to a new room when it's available.
   b) explain that this is not an option for them.
   c) do nothing; this is not uncommon in long-term care.
   d) report their request to the nurse.

6. Client bathrooms in a long-term care facility must be
   a) in each client room.
   b) shared by no more than two clients.
   c) accessible to all clients.
   d) equipped with a tub and a shower.

7. Maria is one of the clients you care for at a long-term care facility. Maria tells you that they have not been able to sleep because their roommate has a lot of family who visit in the evening. You should
   a) move Maria to a new room.
   b) move their roommate to a new room.
   c) ask the family if they can visit in the common room.
   d) tell the family to visit during the day instead.

Name _____

8. A client may be discharged from a long-term care facility if they

   a) are unable to pay for services.
   b) are disrespectful to staff.
   c) make inappropriate comments.
   d) report a staff member to the ombudsman.

9. A discharge notice from a long-term care facility must contain all of the following EXCEPT

   a) the reason for the discharge.
   b) the client's bank account information.
   c) readmission policies of the current facility.
   d) contact information for the ombudsman.

10. A pleasant homelike environment in a healthcare facility can improve

    a) client comfort.
    b) consumer use of the facility.
    c) customer satisfaction.
    d) all of the above.

11. Long-term care facilities try to exceed the minimum requirements listed in OBRA so that they can

    a) attract the savvy healthcare customer.
    b) avoid paying penalties.
    c) charge for additional services.
    d) offer more private rooms.

13.E Choose the best response to the following scenarios.

1. Your client uses the call-light system every 10 minutes and you are getting frustrated. What should you do?

   a) Take the call light away from the client.
   b) Continue to answer the call light every time it is on.
   c) Tell the supervisor to move the client to another room.
   d) Call the client's family and ask them to come to see the client.

2. You are working the night shift and notice many of your coworkers are talking and laughing very loudly. What should you do?

   a) Remind them that the clients are asleep.
   b) Join in—the clients are hard of hearing.
   c) Call the supervisor and complain.
   d) Make sure all of the clients' doors are shut.

3. Two clients share a room. One client is eating breakfast in the room, and their roommate is asking to use the bedside commode. What would you do?

   a) Pull the privacy curtain and place the client on the commode.
   b) Explain that the roommate is eating and take the client to a restroom.
   c) Tell the client that they need to wait until the roommate is finished with breakfast.
   d) Cover the breakfast tray while the commode is being used.

4. Your client is upset and tells you they are being "kicked out" of the nursing home. What is the best response?

   a) Talk to the nurse on their behalf, as there is no need for this.
   b) Contact their family to help make the moving arrangements.
   c) Reassure them that they have a 30-day notice of discharge and someone will help them.
   d) All of the above.

5. Your client is upset because their sister is able to reside at the assisted-living center in town and they must remain at the nursing home. What is the best response?

   a) Explain that it is because they do not have the money to stay at the assisted-living center.
   b) Tell them to call their sister and see if it would be possible for them to share a room.
   c) Encourage the client to call their ombudsman to get this resolved quickly.
   d) Explain that the nursing home can best serve their needs.

64 • Chapter 13

Chapter 14: Preventing Skin Breakdown

14.A Matching Definitions

_____ 1. Bony prominence

_____ 2. Eschar

_____ 3. Debridement

_____ 4. Shear

_____ 5. Friction

_____ 6. Immobility

_____ 7. Microclimate

_____ 8. Maceration

A. The chemical or manual removal of eschar

B. Necrotic tissue sometimes found in a pressure injury

C. The inability of the client to move themselves purposefully

D. Any area of bone that sticks out or protrudes from the body

E. A close environment in which heat and humidity are localized

F. The movement of one layer of skin against another layer, or one layer of skin against a hard surface

G. Skin that is softened from constant exposure to moisture

H. A force on the skin; occurs when the body slides down in bed and the skin sticks to the linens

14.B Reflective Short-Answer Exercises

Carol is a 91-year-old client with diabetes. Carol also has dementia and is incontinent of urine and feces. When you are bathing them today, you notice a red area on their bottom that won't go away. You ask Carol if it hurts them, and they say no. After their bath, you dress them and help them into their wheelchair using a gait belt and assist of another assistant. When you are assisting them with their breakfast, they state they only want to eat desserts.

1. Why do you think Carol might not feel any pain on the reddened area on their bottom?

_____
_____
_____
_____

2. Does Carol have a pressure injury on their bottom? If so, what stage would it be?

_____
_____
_____
_____

Name _____

3. Should you report the reddened area to the nurse? When should you do this?

   _____
   _____
   _____

4. What would put Carol at risk for skin breakdown?

   _____
   _____
   _____
   _____

5. How could Carol's incontinence affect the skin on their bottom?

   _____
   _____
   _____
   _____

6. How often should you be repositioning Carol?

   _____
   _____
   _____
   _____

7. How often should you be changing Carol's incontinence product and performing peri-care?

   _____
   _____
   _____
   _____

8. What product should be used for cleaning the peri-area?

   _____
   _____
   _____
   _____

9. What other interventions can you do to help heal the pressure injury on Carol's bottom?

   _____
   _____
   _____
   _____

10. Would you get Carol extra desserts today and only feed them those? Why or why not?

    _____
    _____
    _____
    _____

66 • Chapter 14

Name _____

14.C Fill in the blanks using terms found in the word bank.

heat	debridement	humidity
shear	rashes	hydration
eschar	immobility	prevention
movement	bone	

1. A bony prominence is any area of _____ that sticks out or protrudes from the body.
2. Necrotic tissue that is sometimes found in the wound bed of a pressure injury is called _____.
3. _____ is the chemical or manual removal of the eschar.
4. Friction is the _____ of one layer of skin against another.
5. _____ is the inability of the client to move themselves purposefully.
6. Microclimate is related to the _____ and _____ between a client's skin and the bed or wheelchair.
7. _____ is the force sliding against an area of the skin.
8. _____ of skin breakdown is your responsibility as a nursing assistant.
9. Sometimes skin _____ are an overgrowth of yeast, causing a yeast infection.
10. _____ and proper protein intake are very important to maintaining healthy skin.

14.D Multiple-Choice Exercises

1. Healthy, intact skin helps to
    a) regulate body temperature.
    b) protect the body from germs.
    c) maintain moisture levels in the body.
    d) do all of the above.

2. Preventable skin rashes most often appear
    a) across the chest and abdomen.
    b) beneath breasts, under arms, and between skin folds.
    c) on the legs and feet.
    d) on the face, neck, and ears.

3. A rash found under a client's arms may be the result of
    a) shearing.
    b) pressure.
    c) infection.
    d) debridement.

4. An intact area on the coccyx that is red, painful, and has edema would be a
    a) stage-one pressure injury.
    b) stage-two pressure injury.
    c) stage-three pressure injury.
    d) stage-four pressure injury.

5. You are assisting a client to the toilet and notice that they have an open area on their coccyx. You should
    a) clean the area and apply barrier cream.
    b) report your findings to the nurse.
    c) place a cushion in the client's wheelchair.
    d) apply a small amount of powder or cornstarch.

6. The factor that places the client MOST at risk of developing a pressure injury is
    a) dementia.
    b) inability to sense pain.
    c) incontinence.
    d) immobility.

7. Ellen is an older client who is immobile and does not have much of an appetite. Because they are at risk of developing pressure injuries, it is MOST important for them to eat

   a) fruits.
   b) grains.
   c) proteins.
   d) vegetables.

8. You are caring for a client in an assisted-living facility. You need to reposition them in bed, but there are no lift sheets available. You should

   a) use a folded top sheet or large towel as a lift sheet.
   b) ask them to pull themself up in bed using the side rails.
   c) reposition them by lifting underneath their arms.
   d) call the nurse and ask them to buy lift sheets.

9. Immobile clients must be repositioned

   a) every 2 hours while in bed.
   b) every hour when in a wheelchair.
   c) every 2 hours while the client is awake.
   d) both a and b.

10. Maceration of a client's skin is likely to result from

    a) repositioning without using a lift sheet.
    b) not changing an incontinence garment when soiled.
    c) not offering snacks and fluids between meals.
    d) placing an alternating-pressure mattress on the bed.

11. The nursing assistant's scope of practice includes

    a) changing sterile bandages.
    b) applying barrier creams to intact skin.
    c) applying prescription ointments to intact skin.
    d) determining the appropriate dressing type for a wound.

14.E Choose the best response to the following scenarios.

1. You notice a reddened area on your client's right heel that was not there yesterday. What should you do FIRST?

   a) Report the pressure injury to the nurse.
   b) Assume that someone else has reported this change.
   c) Place the heel on two pillows.
   d) Watch the area to make sure it does not get worse.

2. While giving your client a bath, you discover a bleeding open wound. What should you do?

   a) Wrap the wound in a dry washcloth and tell the nurse.
   b) Place a clean wet cloth over the area and get the nurse.
   c) Let it bleed until the wound clots.
   d) Use antibiotic ointment and dress the wound.

3. A nursing home client develops a pressure injury. Now the nurse is conducting an investigation. You have provided skin care as directed in the client's care plan. When you are questioned by the nurse, what is your best response?

   a) Explain that it was not your fault, but that your coworkers might be to blame.
   b) Tell the nurse that you have followed the plan of care and that your charting reflects this.
   c) Update the nurse that the client has been eating poorly lately and that this may be the reason for the injury.
   d) Tell the nurse you think the nursing assistants on the night shift are not providing skin care and this is why the client developed the injury.

Name _____

4. Your client's care plan states they should be repositioned every 2 hours. They refuse. What should you do?

   a) Respect their wishes.
   b) Turn them anyway.
   c) Report to the nurse.
   d) Call their family.

5. You notice that your coworker is not offering fluids to the clients, and you're concerned that they may become dehydrated. What should you do?

   a) Make sure you offer extra fluids to make up for it.
   b) Report them to the supervisor immediately.
   c) Understand that this may take extra time that you do not have.
   d) Remind your coworker of the importance of hydration.

This page intentionally left blank.

Chapter 15: Bedmaking

15.A Matching Definitions

_____ 1. Occupied bed change

_____ 2. Bath blanket

_____ 3. Closed bed

_____ 4. Open bed

_____ 5. Linens

_____ 6. Reusable incontinence pad

A. A lightweight blanket used to cover clients for warmth and privacy while providing care

B. A bed made with the top sheet, blanket, and bedspread fanfolded down to the foot or side of the bed

C. A pad that is placed under the incontinent client to protect bed linens

D. The bedding that covers the mattress

E. A bed made with all of the linens in place over the mattress; the top sheet, blanket, and bedspread are drawn up to the head of the bed

F. A change of bed linens when the client is not able to get out of bed, or when it is uncomfortable for the client to get out of bed

15.B Reflective Short-Answer Exercises

Bea is an older client in the assisted-living facility where you work. Normally, they are active. Today they are feeling ill. During the night, they had an incontinent episode while in bed and are clearly upset. Bea needs assistance getting washed but is too weak to get to the bathroom.

1. What type of linen could you use on Bea's bed to prevent another accident from soiling their linens?

   _____
   _____
   _____
   _____

2. What infection-control precautions should you take before changing the linens?

   _____
   _____
   _____
   _____

3. What supplies would you need to gather before you change their linens?

   _____
   _____
   _____
   _____

Name _____

4. How would you change their bed linens so that they remain comfortable?

_____
_____
_____
_____

5. What would you do with the soiled linens from Bea's bed?

_____
_____
_____
_____

15.C Fill in the blanks using terms found in the word bank.

contamination	linens	occupied bed change
housekeeping staff	open bed	dry
lift sheet	bath	privacy
clean	warmth	

1. A bath blanket is used to cover clients for _____ and _____.
2. A bed made with all _____ over the mattress including the fitted sheet, top sheet, blanket, and bedspread drawn up to the head of the bed is called a closed bed.
3. A(n) _____ is a change of bed linens when the client is not able to get out of bed or when it is uncomfortable for the client to get out of bed.
4. A(n) _____ is made with the top sheet, blanket, and bedspread fanfolded down to the foot of the bed.
5. Linens should be gathered in the correct order and kept away from the body to avoid _____.
6. It is the nursing assistant's responsibility to keep the client's skin healthy by ensuring the bed linens are _____ and _____.
7. A(n) _____ is used when moving the client up in the bed or over to the side of the bed during positioning.
8. In assisted-living and long-term care facilities, bed linens are changed once or twice each week, on the same day as the client's _____.
9. Either the nursing assistant or the _____ is responsible for changing the client's linens.

Name _____

15.D Multiple-Choice Exercises

1. You are changing the linens on an alternating-pressure bed for a client who is incontinent. What should you place on the bed to prevent the bed linens from becoming soiled?

    a) reusable incontinence pad
    b) mattress pad
    c) disposable incontinence pad
    d) draw sheet

2. Mattress pads are NEVER used in

    a) hospitals.
    b) home health.
    c) assisted-living facilities.
    d) residential care apartment complexes.

3. You gather linens to change Sarah's bed. After you are in Sarah's room, you notice that you brought an extra fitted sheet. What should you do with the extra sheet?

    a) Return it to the linen closet.
    b) Place it in the soiled linen bag.
    c) Take it to the next client's room to use.
    d) Set it on the floor while you make the bed.

4. When changing bed linens, the nursing assistant MUST wear gloves

    a) only when removing linens that are wet.
    b) when putting new linens on the bed.
    c) when removing any linens from the bed.
    d) during none of the above.

5. When making an occupied bed, the nursing assistant should have the bed

    a) at about waist height.
    b) in the lowest position.
    c) against the wall.
    d) unlocked when rolling the client.

6. Good body mechanics include all of the following EXCEPT

    a) raising the bed to a good working height.
    b) keeping items close to your body.
    c) lowering side rails while you work.
    d) bending at the waist.

7. When a client is ready to go to bed, the linens should be

    a) fanfolded to one side of the bed.
    b) fanfolded to the bottom of the bed.
    c) rolled down to the bottom of the bed.
    d) drawn up to the head of the bed.

8. The nursing assistant should make a closed bed when a client is

    a) admitted to the hospital.
    b) ready to get into bed.
    c) up for the day.
    d) transferred from a stretcher.

9. While you are making an occupied bed, the side rails should be raised

    a) on the side the client is rolling toward.
    b) on the side where you are working.
    c) never; side rails are a restraint.
    d) on both sides until you are finished.

10. You need to make an occupied bed for one of your clients. The bed does not have side rails. What should you do?

    a) Make the bed while it is in the low position.
    b) Roll the client toward you while making the bed.
    c) Tell the client that they have to get out of bed.
    d) Move the bed against the wall and reach over the client.

15.E Choose the best response to the following scenarios.

1. Your client tells you they do not want the incontinence pad placed on their bed even though you know they are incontinent at night. What should you do?

    a) Place the pad there anyway to ensure the linens remain clean.
    b) Explain the importance of the protector in keeping their skin healthy.
    c) Use a bath blanket instead of the bed protector.
    d) Warn your coworkers that the linens will become soiled during the night.

2. Your client is watching you make their bed and is becoming very upset because you do not make the bed the way your coworker does. What should you do?

    a) Ask the client to explain to you how they would like their bed made.
    b) Ask your coworker to make the bed the way the client likes it.
    c) Ask the nurse to make the bed; they are better at mitered corners.
    d) Ask the client to make their own bed.

3. One of your clients has had an incontinent episode while in bed. You gather clean linens and begin an occupied bed change when the client's roommate enters the room. What should you do?

    a) Tell the roommate that they must remain in the hall until you say they may enter.
    b) Ignore the roommate and continue with the bed change.
    c) Ask the roommate if they would be able to wait in the hall until you are done.
    d) Turn on the call light and ask the nurse to change the linens for you.

4. You are stripping a dirty bed with your gloves on and realize you forgot a top sheet when you collected the linens. What should you do?

    a) Keep the gloves on and go get the top sheet.
    b) Put a pair of clean gloves over the dirty pair before getting the top sheet.
    c) Make the bed without the top sheet; you will remember to do that later.
    d) Remove your gloves, wash hands, and retrieve a top sheet.

5. Your client tells you they want their bed linens changed every day, but the facility recommends they are changed only on bath day. What should you do?

    a) Change the bed only on bath day as per the facility policy.
    b) Report the request to the supervisor so the client's care plan can be updated.
    c) Tell the client that you will change the bed daily, but do not do it.
    d) Compromise and change the bed three times a week.

Chapter 16: Positioning, Moving, and Transporting Clients

16.A Matching Definitions

____ 1. Gait belt

____ 2. Trapeze

____ 3. Friction/shearing prevention device

A. An implement that attaches to the bed frame, extending out overhead and used for leverage by the client for repositioning in bed

B. A device used to move clients with the least amount of friction or shearing on the client and the least amount of exertion for the nursing assistant

C. A device placed around the client's waist for use when transferring and ambulating

16.B Reflective Short-Answer Exercises

Yvonne is a bariatric client who has a stage 3 pressure injury on their sacrum. They are expected to be out of bed at meal times. Their care plan states that they need to be transferred with a two-person assist, a gait belt, and a walker.

1. Why do you think it is important to get Yvonne up and out of bed for meals?

2. You must reposition Yvonne in bed every 2 hours throughout your shift. What supplies could you use to assist with moving Yvonne up in bed?

3. What interventions could you use to assist them with sitting on the side of the bed, without physically lifting them up?

4. If Yvonne was not feeling well, or could not follow your directives to stand, how could you safely transfer them into their wheelchair for breakfast?

Name _____

16.C Fill in the blanks using terms found in the word bank.

tripod	sleeping	semi-Fowler's
shearing	ligament	waist
flat	safety	bed frame
Fowler's	transferring	Sims's
repositioned	muscles	trochanter roll

1. Clients must be _____ every 2 hours while in bed and every 1 hour while in a wheelchair.

2. The head of the bed must be _____ before moving the client up in the bed.

3. _____ is a form of side-lying position used when a client needs an enema.

4. The supine position is a comfortable _____ position for most people.

5. The nursing assistant assumes a wide stance and uses the large _____ of the hips, thighs, and buttocks during the client movement to prevent injury to themselves.

6. A contracture is the physical shortening of a _____.

7. Placing shoes or nonskid slippers on a client's feet during client transfers is a very important _____ consideration.

8. The head of the bed is raised to about 35–40 degrees in the _____ position.

9. The head of the bed is raised to anywhere between 45 and 60 degrees for the _____ position.

10. _____ across the bed linens during repositioning should be limited as much as possible.

11. A _____ is a cushion or device to keep the client's hip, leg, and foot in a neutral position.

12. Often, clients who suffer from respiratory disorders assume a _____ position.

13. A gait belt is a device placed around the client's _____ during transferring and ambulating to keep the client safe.

14. A trapeze is an implement that attaches to the _____ and is used for leverage by the client to reposition in bed.

15. A gait belt is a device that is used when _____ or ambulating a client to keep the client and the nursing assistant free from injury.

Name _____

16.D Multiple-Choice Exercises

1. What position would a client with breathing problems be most comfortable in?

   a) prone
   b) supine
   c) Sims's
   d) Fowler's

2. The nurse tells you that Stanley needs to have an enema. What position should you place them in?

   a) Sims's
   b) supine
   c) semi-Fowler's
   d) prone

3. To place a client in a semi-Fowler's position, the head of the bed should be

   a) raised 45–60 degrees.
   b) raised 35–40 degrees.
   c) raised 80–90 degrees.
   d) left flat.

4. The position that puts a client at greatest risk of shearing injuries to the back, sacrum, and coccyx is

   a) supine.
   b) high-Fowler's.
   c) side-lying.
   d) semi-Fowler's.

5. Positioning a client properly in a wheelchair helps to

   a) prevent pressure injuries.
   b) decrease discomfort.
   c) reduce the risk of a fall.
   d) do all of the above.

6. Anna is an older client with very fragile skin. They need to be moved up in bed. The BEST device to use in assisting Anna is a:

   a) draw sheet.
   b) trapeze.
   c) back board.
   d) friction/shearing prevention device.

7. Freida's care plan states that they need an alternating-pressure pad in their wheelchair. When you place the pad in the wheelchair, Freida is unable to put their feet flat on the floor. You should

   a) talk with the nurse about the wheelchair size.
   b) leave the pad out of the chair so that they can move about.
   c) search the facility for a different wheelchair.
   d) reposition them so that they sit further forward.

8. Before log rolling a client, a pillow needs to be placed:

   a) under the client's legs.
   b) between the client's legs.
   c) under each of the client's arms.
   d) behind the client's hips.

9. When a client is in Fowler's position, pillows must be placed

   a) under the head only.
   b) under the head and upper arms.
   c) under the head and lower legs.
   d) behind the knees.

10. One nursing assistant can move a client up in bed if

    a) the client has no side rails on their bed.
    b) the client has a trapeze secured to the bed.
    c) the client grabs the nursing assistant's arms for support.
    d) none of the above; repositioning requires a two assist.

11. When two nursing assistants move a client up in bed, they should grasp the draw sheet

    a) 4 inches away from the client's body.
    b) 6 inches away from the client's body.
    c) as close to the client's body as possible.
    d) as far from the client's body as possible.

12. John is an older client who has a colostomy. John's care plan states that they transfer with an assist of one and a gait belt. Their colostomy prevents you from placing the gait belt around John's waist. You should transfer them by

    a) using a mechanical lift.
    b) placing the gait belt above the colostomy.
    c) lifting under their arms.
    d) using a pivot disc instead of the gait belt.

13. The FIRST step in transferring a client from bed to a wheelchair is to

    a) place the wheelchair at the foot of the bed.
    b) remove the leg rests from the wheelchair.
    c) tell the client what you need them to do.
    d) check the client's care plan or ISP.

14. For repositioning a bariatric client while in bed, you need to

    a) ask for help from at least one other coworker.
    b) use a top sheet, bath blanket, or bed blanket.
    c) ask the client to help as much as they are able.
    d) do all of the above.

15. You are transporting a client in their wheelchair. Their feet drag on the floor because they are unable to keep them lifted while you are moving. You should

    a) place a cushion under their buttocks to keep their feet from touching the floor.
    b) place leg rests on the wheelchair if indicated on the client's care plan.
    c) have a coworker hold their legs up while you transport the client.
    d) pull the wheelchair backward so their feet do not get hurt.

16. Sarah is a client who has leg rests on their wheelchair to keep their legs elevated. You help them to their room after dinner because they are unable to propel themself. Before leaving Sarah's room, you should

    a) remove the leg rests and hand them the call light.
    b) move the leg rests out to the side of their chair.
    c) keep the leg rests on as indicated on their care plan.
    d) do none of the above.

17. A friction and shearing prevention device is used:

    a) to prevent staff back injuries.
    b) to protect a client's fragile skin.
    c) to more easily move an obese client.
    d) all of the above.

18. Before transferring a client from bed to stretcher, you must raise the bed until it is:

    a) the same height as the stretcher.
    b) 2 inches lower than the stretcher.
    c) at the same level as your waist.
    d) 2 inches higher than the stretcher.

Name _____

16.E Choose the best response to the following scenarios.

1. Your client has been up in their wheelchair for 2 hours and does not want to lie in bed or sit in their recliner. Their care plan says to reposition them every 2 hours. What should you do?

    a) Help them to stand or ambulate.
    b) Put them in the recliner in the sun room.
    c) Help them back to the bed.
    d) Place them in front of the television.

2. You are instructed to reposition your client with three pillows. You only have two. What should you do?

    a) Use only the two that you have.
    b) Borrow one of the roommate's pillows.
    c) Call the family to purchase more pillows.
    d) Roll a bath blanket to use as a positioning device.

3. You find your client in the tripod position, and they refuse to reposition. Why might they be in this position?

    a) They have breathing problems.
    b) They are going to have an enema.
    c) They are watching television from bed.
    d) They have a pressure injury on their coccyx.

4. Your client refuses to allow you to use the gait belt as the care plan states. What should you do?

    a) Respect your client's wishes and do not use the gait belt.
    b) Ask another nursing assistant to complete the transfer.
    c) Reinforce to the client the importance of using the gait belt and report to the supervisor.
    d) Call the patient's family and inform them that the client is refusing to use the gait belt.

5. Your client's care plan states to use a pivot disk during transfers, but you have not been instructed on the proper use of the disk. What should you do?

    a) Use a walker instead; you saw a coworker do this earlier.
    b) Ask your supervisor for instruction.
    c) Read the instructions on the pivot disk prior to use.
    d) Ask the physical therapist to transfer the client.

6. You are asked to boost a bariatric client up in bed. What should you do?

    a) Obtain enough assistance from staff to ensure that you do not injure your back.
    b) Do your best to boost the bariatric client by yourself; they also have a trapeze to assist.
    c) Tell the client that you are unable to perform this task.
    d) Use a mechanical lift to move the client upward in bed.

7. Your client is doing well and seems to be able to transfer with two assist instead of the mechanical lift as the care plan states. What should you do?

    a) Transfer the client with two assist so that they regain strength.
    b) Use the mechanical lift and report your findings to the supervisor.
    c) Transfer the client with two assist and the gait belt for added safety.
    d) Ask your coworkers how they transferred the client.

This page intentionally left blank.

Chapter 17: Ambulation, Restorative Care, and Adaptive Equipment for Clients

17.A Matching Definitions

_____ 1. Mastectomy

_____ 2. Orthosis

_____ 3. Passive range of motion

_____ 4. Apraxia

_____ 5. Dysarthria

_____ 6. Laryngectomy

_____ 7. IADLs

_____ 8. Prosthesis

_____ 9. Active range of motion

_____ 10. ADLs

A. Exercises in which the client is actively participating and is moving the joint themself

B. The partial or complete removal of a breast

C. Exercises in which the nursing assistant is physically moving the client's joint

D. Impaired speech muscles, causing difficulty in forming words

E. Activities of daily life that require the use of instruments, tools, or appliances

F. Nervous system disorder in which a person is unable to perform a task when asked to do so

G. An artificial limb or body part

H. The removal of the larynx

I. A brace, splint, or orthopedic device; sometimes called an orthotic

J. Activities related to daily care like movement and transferring, bathing, dressing, and using the restroom

17.B Reflective Short-Answer Exercises

Trudy is a client recovering from a recent stroke. They are in the facility trying to regain strength and the function of their right side. You need to assist them with walking to the dining room. They become angry when you put the gait belt around their waist; they don't like it. While you are helping them walk, they become weak and almost fall. You sit them back down in the wheelchair and wheel them into the dining room.

1. What benefits would Trudy gain by ambulating to the dining room for each meal?

_____
_____
_____

2. What level of assistance do you think Trudy might need with ambulation?

_____
_____
_____

Name _____

3. Trudy's care plan states they are to ambulate with an assist of one. Can you get more help and use two nursing assistants to walk them to the dining room?

_____
_____
_____
_____

4. What safety interventions must you consider before ambulating Trudy?

_____
_____
_____
_____

5. What assistive devices might help to steady Trudy during ambulation?

_____
_____
_____
_____

6. What else besides ambulation could help Trudy prevent a contracture from their stroke?

_____
_____
_____
_____

17.C Fill in the blanks using terms found in the word bank.

safety	ambulation	digestive system
cardiovascular	skin	moving
rubber-tipped spoon	family members	occupational therapist
maximize	physical therapist	nursing assistant

1. Occupational therapy services always involve the client, but may also involve _____ and caretakers.

2. It is very important that the nursing assistant look at the _____ beneath the prosthesis at least two times per day.

3. The goal of _____ exercise, such as walking and running, is to keep the heart strong and working properly.

4. _____ is very important when ambulating clients to prevent injury.

5. Passive range of motion (PROM) is when the _____ physically moves the client's joints through the exercise. The client does not assist in the movement, or assists very little.

6. The goal of therapy services is to restore prior ability or to _____ potential.

7. Walking and other types of movement help the motility in the _____ to prevent constipation.

8. The _____ initially evaluates the client for meeting rehabilitation needs and works with the client in improving large, gross motor skills.

9. The nursing assistant should use a _____ to prevent breakage by clients who have a reflex of biting down on items in the mouth.

10. Part of a nursing assistant's job is to help clients with _____ and _____.

11. The _____ is responsible for evaluating clients with a variety of disorders and is geared toward improving fine motor skills such as handling and manipulating small objects, like keys, dials, and buttons.

17.D Multiple-Choice Exercises

1. Assisting a client with ambulation helps
   a) reduce leg and feet swelling.
   b) prevent contractures.
   c) maintain muscle tone.
   d) do all of the above.

2. You can assist the client who is independent with ambulation by
   a) telling them they must walk to the dining room for meals.
   b) encouraging them to attend group activities offered that day.
   c) not allowing them to use a wheelchair.
   d) remaining close to them when they walk.

3. Juan's care plan states that they are a one assist. To assist in ambulation, you will need to
   a) use a gait belt with at least one hand on it at all times.
   b) ask another nursing assistant to help you.
   c) give them verbal reminders to walk each day.
   d) use a gait belt only if they are feeling weak or unsteady.

4. Before you assist a client to stand, they must be wearing
   a) shoes or have bare feet.
   b) socks or bathroom slippers.
   c) footwear with a nonskid sole.
   d) what they find most comfortable.

5. Moving an arm or leg away from the midline of the body is called
   a) flexion.
   b) abduction.
   c) dorsiflexion.
   d) adduction.

6. You notice that Christian has recently needed more assistance with tasks like brushing their teeth and shaving. You should
   a) alert the nurse and continue to encourage independence.
   b) update the physical and occupational therapists.
   c) do nothing; this is a normal part of aging.
   d) shave and brush their teeth for them so they don't become frustrated.

7. A client who has just received a prosthetic hand would MOST likely need
   a) speech therapy.
   b) a restorative aide.
   c) occupational therapy.
   d) activities therapy.

8. The nursing assistant must check the skin beneath a brace:
   a) only before putting the brace on.
   b) while the client is wearing the brace.
   c) before and after placing the brace on the client.
   d) only when the client complains of discomfort or pain.

Name _____

9. Lawrence is an older client with Parkinson's disease. They find it hard to feed themselves due to shaky hands. The adaptive device that would BEST increase their independence during meal times is a

   a) straw.
   b) covered cup.
   c) nonskid mat.
   d) plate guard.

10. Activities therapy may include

    a) treatment for a client's pressure injury.
    b) helping a client put together a jigsaw puzzle.
    c) showing a client how to safely climb stairs.
    d) none of the above.

11. Dwayne is a client who has had a recent hip replacement and should not bend forward at the hip. An adaptive device that might help them be more independent when dressing is a

    a) button aid.
    b) toilet seat riser.
    c) sock aid.
    d) elastic shoelaces.

12. Claire is a long-term care client who needs to be ambulated twice a day. The person responsible for this would be the

    a) restorative aide.
    b) charge nurse.
    c) activities director.
    d) occupational therapist.

13. You are performing range-of-motion exercises on Agatha's knee. They wince in pain with the movement. You should

    a) stop the exercises and inform the nurse that Agatha is having pain.
    b) let Agatha rest for five minutes and then try again.
    c) continue with the exercises to help loosen the muscles.
    d) skip range-of-motion exercises for the day.

14. Harold is an 85-year-old client with dementia who needs daily care. They are easily confused with simple tasks and had a history of wandering when they lived at home. An appropriate activity for Harold would be

    a) shopping at a local mall.
    b) a trip to a craft fair.
    c) an ice cream social.
    d) participating in a book club.

15. The nursing assistant must check the skin beneath a client's prosthesis

    a) once a week on bath day.
    b) at least once every three days.
    c) before placing and after removal of the prosthesis.
    d) once per day in the morning.

16. When applying a warm compress, the application should be applied to the area for:

    a) 30 minutes.
    b) 10–15 minutes.
    c) 20 minutes.
    d) 5 minutes.

17.E Choose the best response to the following scenarios.

1. While you are ambulating Jamar, they fall and you are able to safely lower them to the ground. Jamar says they are all right and not hurt. What should you do?

   a) Help Jamar stand and continue to ambulate.
   b) Ask a coworker for assistance to continue ambulating.
   c) Get the supervisor before moving the client.
   d) Get the mechanical lift and lift Jamar to a chair.

2. Your client has fallen in the past and is scared to ambulate. What would you do?

   a) Do not ambulate the client if they are afraid.
   b) Tell them that it is required for good health.
   c) Provide encouragement to walk small amounts at a time.
   d) Call their family and ask that they walk them.

3. Ibrahim has asked you to help them to the toilet. While you are trying to put a gait belt around Ibrahim for this transfer, they say, "I need to go now," and then tries to stand up alone. What should you do?

   a) Let Ibrahim stand up and ambulate without the gait belt.
   b) Stand in front of Ibrahim while applying the gait belt and remind them of safety.
   c) Refuse to help Ibrahim because they are being unreasonable.
   d) Leave Ibrahim in the restroom and get the supervisor.

4. You notice your client having difficulty swallowing. You update the nurse. What would you expect to happen next?

   a) A speech therapist would assess the client.
   b) A physical therapist would assess the client.
   c) An occupational therapist would assess the client.
   d) The nurse would ask family members to feed the client at meal times.

5. Your client is self-conscious regarding their prosthetic eye and asks for privacy while placing it. What should you do?

   a) Leave the room but keep the door open in case they need help.
   b) Pull the privacy curtain, make sure they have the call light, and leave the room.
   c) Reassure them that you have seen this before and tell them that you can help if needed.
   d) None of the above; they should not do this themself.

6. Dante is having a hard time using the utensils at meal time due to swollen joints from arthritis. What should you do?

   a) Feed Dante their meals and snacks.
   b) Let Dante eat with their fingers.
   c) Offer Dante small bites.
   d) Provide assistive devices for meals.

This page intentionally left blank.

Name _____

Chapter 18: Vital Signs

18.A Matching Definitions

_____ 1. Bradycardia
_____ 2. Tachypnea
_____ 3. Korotkoff sound
_____ 4. Bradypnea
_____ 5. Hypertension
_____ 6. Tachycardia
_____ 7. Hypotension
_____ 8. Lymphedema

A. Blood pressure that is too high; measurements are higher than 140/90 mmHg

B. Breathing that is too fast; respirations are greater than 20 breaths per minute

C. A high heart rate

D. Blood pressure that is too low; typically any measurements lower than 90/60 mmHg

E. Slow breathing; respirations are less than 12 breaths per minute

F. Painful swelling

G. Heartbeats heard through the stethoscope while taking blood pressure

H. A low heart rate

18.B Reflective Short-Answer Exercises

You work in an assisted-living facility and are caring for Herman tonight. While you are walking with them, they pass out and fall. You call 911 and take vital signs, which you report to the emergency team when they arrive. Their temperature is 99.9°F, taken axillary, pulse is 108, respirations are 14, and blood pressure is 190/98.

1. Was it an appropriate time to take a set of vital signs on Herman? Why or why not?

_____
_____
_____
_____

2. What would you need to do with the vital sign equipment after using it on Herman?

_____
_____
_____
_____

3. Was Herman's temperature normal? What is the normal range for temperature?

_____
_____
_____
_____

4. Was Herman's pulse within normal limits? What is the normal range for an adult's pulse?

_____
_____
_____
_____

5. Were Herman's respirations within normal limits? What is the normal range for respirations?

_____
_____
_____
_____

6. Was Herman's blood pressure within normal limits? What is the normal range for blood pressure?

_____
_____
_____
_____

18.C Fill in the blanks using terms found in the word bank.

tachypnea   pulse oximetry   stethoscope
sixty   hypertension   non-contact infrared thermometer
painful   tachycardia   hypotension
bradypnea

1. Bradycardia is a heart rate less than _____ beats per minute.
2. _____ is slow breathing, less than 12 breaths per minute.
3. Blood pressure that is too high is called _____.
4. A blood pressure reading less than 90/60 is called _____.
5. _____ is the least invasive way to take a temperature as there is no contact with the client at all.
6. Lymphedema is a _____ swelling of the arm.
7. Breathing that is too fast and typically shallow is called _____.
8. The Korotkoff sound is heart beats heard via a _____ while taking blood pressure.
9. A heart rate of greater than 100 beats per minute is called _____.
10. _____ measures oxygen levels in the blood, also known as oxygen saturation.

Name _____

18.D Multiple-Choice Exercises

1. Height is usually measured

    a) when a client is admitted to the facility.
    b) once a year on the annual admission date.
    c) each time weight is measured on bath day.
    d) at none of these times.

2. The client likely to have their vital signs taken MOST often would be a(n)

    a) 80-year-old client who fell a week ago.
    b) 76-year-old client admitted to the hospital with pneumonia.
    c) 24-year-old home health client with Down syndrome.
    d) 82-year-old client with dementia living in an assisted-living facility.

3. You have a client who is in contact isolation due to infection. A full set of vital sign equipment for the client needs to be kept

    a) in the client's room.
    b) right outside the client's door.
    c) at the nurse's desk.
    d) in the dirty supply closet.

4. To prevent the spread of infection, vital sign equipment must be

    a) kept in all client rooms.
    b) cleaned with alcohol after each use.
    c) used once and then discarded.
    d) cleaned with soap and water before each use.

5. The average temperature taken with a tympanic thermometer is

    a) 98.6°F.
    b) 99.6°F.
    c) 96.6°F.
    d) 97.6°F.

6. The method that is least invasive and most accurate for obtaining a temperature is

    a) axillary.
    b) rectal.
    c) temporal.
    d) oral.

18.E Choose the best response to the following scenarios.

1. Your task is to obtain vital signs on seven clients. You are going from room to room taking vital signs. You obtain the vital signs of your fifth client and they are abnormal. What should you do?

    a) Continue to take the last two sets of vital signs and then report the abnormal set to the nurse.
    b) After retaking the vital signs to confirm they are abnormal, report to the nurse right away and then continue to take the last two sets.
    c) Take the last two sets and then report all of the vital signs taken to the nurse at the end of the shift.
    d) Immediately report the abnormal vital signs to the nurse and then continue to take the last two sets.

2. Your client's blood pressure is 240/230 after taking the blood pressure reading twice with the electronic wrist blood pressure cuff. Your client says they feel fine. What should you do?

    a) Report to the nurse and ask them to obtain a reading with a stethoscope and sphygmomanometer.
    b) Assume the electronic blood pressure cuff is correct and tell the nurse there is an emergency situation.
    c) Request that the nurse transport the client to the emergency room immediately.
    d) Assume the electronic cuff is broken and report this to the nurse at the end of shift.

Name _____

3. Miriam refuses to let you weigh them. What should you do?
   a) Report the client's refusal to the nurse right away.
   b) Reassure Miriam that you have obtained the weight of clients a lot larger than they are.
   c) Ask the nurse to get Miriam's weight, as they have a better relationship with the client.
   d) Respect Miriam's wishes and reattempt to obtain their weight the next morning.

4. Your nursing assistant training did not include instruction on how to properly take a blood pressure, and you are now required to do this. What should you do?
   a) Get your textbook and read the chapter on how to take a blood pressure.
   b) Politely inform the nurse that it is not within your scope of practice.
   c) Let the other nursing assistants take all of the blood pressures.
   d) Ask your immediate supervisor to take the blood pressures.

Name _____

Chapter 19: Bathing

19.A Definitions

In your own words, write a definition for the following terms.

1. Peri-care:
   _____
   _____

2. Paraphimosis:
   _____
   _____

19.B Reflective Short-Answer Exercises

Ida is a resident at the long-term care facility where you work. The last few days Ida has not been feeling well due to a urinary tract infection. Their symptoms of dementia are much more prominent. You are assigned to assist Ida with their bath this morning. Normally, Ida enjoys their bath, but when you try to take them into the tub room, they start screaming and crying.

1. Why would Ida's bath be disturbing to them now when it has been a source of comfort in the past?
   _____
   _____
   _____
   _____

2. Should you continue with Ida's bath despite their behavior? Why or why not?
   _____
   _____
   _____
   _____

3. What alternatives could you use to limit Ida's distress during bathing?
   _____
   _____
   _____
   _____

4. How should you wash Ida's hair to minimize distress?
   _____
   _____
   _____
   _____

Name _____

5. What other responsibilities do you have when caring for Ida today?

_____
_____
_____
_____

19.C Fill in the blanks using terms found in the word bank.

alternatives	supplies	partially bathed
back rub	room	challenge
privacy	rinseless	skin
urethra	showers or tub baths	client
empathetic	perineal	

1. Before beginning the bath, prepare a clean and easily accessible space on which to place your _____.
2. Peri-care is washing the _____ area.
3. The nursing assistant must adapt bathing techniques to meet the needs and desires of the _____.
4. Each client should be _____ twice each day with the exception of their shower or tub bath day.
5. It is important to always check the client's _____ while bathing.
6. Client bathing can be a _____ for those who have dementia.
7. During bathing, be _____ and sincere in your caring so that the client is more comfortable.
8. Always provide _____ when bathing a client.
9. There are _____ to traditional tub bathing or showering that can make bathing more comfortable for clients with dementia.
10. _____ soap is an effective, efficient, and gentle way to cleanse clients.
11. After you have finished bathing and grooming the client, you must tidy the client's _____.
12. Rinseless shampoo is an excellent alternative for individuals who need or want their hair washed but cannot tolerate _____.
13. The _____ is the cleanest part of the perineum.
14. A _____ is a nice way to decrease tension, sooth aching muscles, and calm the client.

Name _____

19.D Multiple-Choice Exercises

1. Peri-care should be completed

    a) each morning when the client wakes.
    b) every evening before going to bed.
    c) after changing a soiled incontinence garment.
    d) all of the above.

2. Lotion should NOT be applied to a client's

    a) feet.
    b) back.
    c) abdominal folds.
    d) chest.

3. Coral is scheduled to have their shower this morning. Coral often gets cold during their shower, but there are no clean bath blankets available. You should

    a) use a bed blanket to cover Coral during the shower.
    b) wait for the laundry service to bring clean bath blankets.
    c) ask the next shift to give Coral their shower.
    d) explain to Coral that you will finish the shower as quickly as possible to avoid chilling them.

4. Javier often becomes upset and agitated when given their weekly shower. Javier finds it cold and painful. You should

    a) offer a complete bed bath in place of the shower.
    b) keep Javier covered with a bath blanket or towels.
    c) provide a partial bed bath instead of a shower.
    d) both a and b.

5. Bathing with a rinseless system instead of soap and water

    a) is more time consuming.
    b) can be gentler on the client's skin.
    c) means the skin is not as clean.
    d) is not appropriate for older clients.

6. You are getting James ready this morning. While you are completing peri-care, James makes a sexual remark that makes you uncomfortable. You should

    a) laugh at the remark to show that you are not bothered by it.
    b) ignore the remark and continue with their morning care.
    c) tell James in a professional tone that this type of talk is unacceptable.
    d) have another nursing assistant finish the bath for you.

7. Peri-care for clients with female anatomy should be completed by cleansing the area from

    a) front to back, starting at the urethra.
    b) front to back, starting with the groin and upper thigh.
    c) back to front, starting at the urethra.
    d) back to front, starting with the anus.

8. A partial bed bath includes all of the following areas of the body EXCEPT

    a) under breasts.
    b) the peri-area.
    c) under abdominal folds.
    d) arms.

9. A complete bed bath typically begins with the client's

    a) hands.
    b) face.
    c) chest.
    d) peri-area.

10. When assisting with a client's shower, you should wash the hair

    a) first, and then proceed to the face and body.
    b) last, so the client does not get cold.
    c) either first or last, whichever the client prefers.
    d) none of the above; all clients have their hair done in the beauty shop.

11. The water temperature of a whirlpool tub bath should be between

    a) 100°F and 104°F.
    b) 90°F and 100°F.
    c) 75°F and 85°F.
    d) 105°F and 110°F.

12. For a client who takes a whirlpool tub bath, peri-care is completed

    a) in their room before the tub bath.
    b) while they are in the tub by stooping next to them.
    c) by the jet action of the whirlpool tub.
    d) none of the above; peri-care is not done.

13. Maria is a client who becomes cold and upset when you wash their hair during their shower. You can decrease Maria's discomfort by

    a) washing Maria's hair as quickly as possible.
    b) shampooing Maria's hair using a trough in bed.
    c) using a rinseless shampoo while Maria is dressed.
    d) both b and c.

14. On a client's bath day, the nursing assistant is also responsible for

    a) obtaining the client's weight.
    b) changing the linens on the client's bed.
    c) providing nail care.
    d) all of the above.

19.E Choose the best response to the following scenarios.

1. Your client's partner says they would prefer to bathe their husband. What is the best response?

    a) Do not allow this, as they are not properly trained.
    b) Tell them that you prefer to do the bathing.
    c) Let them bathe them, but do it again when they go home.
    d) Report the request to the nurse and ask for directives.

2. After many attempts, your client still refuses to take a tub bath. What should you do?

    a) Offer an alternative such as a bed bath.
    b) Do nothing; they have the right to refuse.
    c) Ask a coworker to complete the bath for you.
    d) Ask the nurse to change their bath day.

3. You are working the 7:00 a.m. to 3:00 p.m. shift today. At noon, a new client from the hospital is admitted to your facility. They are very unkempt and dirty. What should you do?

    a) Wait until evening to complete a partial bath.
    b) Take the client for a tub bath or shower.
    c) Let the client use a rinseless soap to wash themselves.
    d) Complain that the hospital staff is lazy.

4. Dora is incontinent and has had a large loose bowel movement in their incontinence garment while at the breakfast table. What should you do?

    a) Allow Dora to finish breakfast in the dining room and then take Dora to their room to provide peri-care.
    b) Take Dora and their breakfast to their room and perform peri-care when they are done eating breakfast.
    c) Discreetly take Dora to their room, provide peri-care, and then assist them back to the dining room.
    d) Allow Dora to finish breakfast and then do peri-care within the next hour.

5. You are given only two washcloths to complete the client's partial bed bath. What should you do?

    a) Starting at the top of the client's body, wash downward, being sure to perform peri-care last.
    b) Reuse the washcloths from yesterday's bath.
    c) Use another client's clean washcloths.
    d) Use paper towel from the dispenser to dry the skin.

Name _____

Chapter 20: Grooming

20.A Matching Definitions

_____ 1. Orange stick

_____ 2. Alopecia

_____ 3. Oral swab

_____ 4. TED hose

A. Tight, elastic stockings designed to prevent blood clots from forming in the legs

B. A small wooden stick with a pointed end and a wedged flat end; used for cleaning beneath the nails

C. A sponge attached to a small stick; used to clean the inside of the mouth

D. A loss of body hair, usually on the scalp

20.B Reflective Short-Answer Exercises

Izetta is a 63-year-old who recently suffered a stroke. They now have right-sided weakness, partial blindness in their right eye, and swallowing problems. Izetta is admitted to a long-term care facility for physical, occupational, and speech therapy. Izetta will need assistance with tasks, including grooming.

1. How could you help Izetta but still preserve their self-esteem?

_____
_____
_____

2. How would you put on Izetta's shirt, given their right-sided weakness?

_____
_____
_____

3. Now that Izetta has partial blindness, they have to get used to wearing glasses. What could you do to help them adjust?

_____
_____
_____

4. What should you do before helping them put their glasses on?

_____
_____
_____

Name _____

20.C Fill in the blanks using terms found in the word bank.

every night	hearing aid	affected
nails	soft cloth	oral swabs
direction	independent	two

1. Disposable sponges attached to a small stick used to clean the inside of the mouth are called _____.

2. An orange stick is a small wooden stick with a sharp pointed end and a wedged flat end used for cleaning beneath the _____.

3. We should encourage clients to be as _____ as possible to maintain strength and mobility.

4. When assisting a client with dressing, you should offer at least _____ outfits for the client to choose between.

5. When dressing a client who suffers from one-sided paralysis, you should always begin by inserting the client's _____ side into the shirt sleeve first.

6. To prevent scratching the lenses, clean glasses with a _____.

7. After inserting the _____ into the ear, ask the client if they can hear you before moving on to the next task.

8. Shave a client's face in the _____ of hair growth when using a disposable razor.

9. Oral care should be performed every morning and _____.

20.D Multiple-Choice Exercises

1. Encouraging your client to perform tasks such as washing the face helps to
   a) maintain muscle mass.
   b) provide range-of-motion exercise.
   c) maintain self-esteem.
   d) do all of the above.

2. After waking, the FIRST thing you typically assist a client with is
   a) getting dressed.
   b) a partial bed bath or shower.
   c) oral care.
   d) range-of-motion exercises.

3. Agnes is a client who has left-sided weakness due to a stroke. When getting Agnes dressed, you should
   a) put their left arm into the sleeve first, while supporting the arm.
   b) put their right arm into the sleeve first.
   c) put their shirt over their head first, followed by their right arm.
   d) put both arms into the sleeves, and then pull the shirt over the head.

4. You should clean a client's eyeglasses by using
   a) hot water and paper towels.
   b) warm water and a soft cloth.
   c) glass cleaner and paper towels.
   d) warm water and facial tissues.

Name _____

5. You have put your client's hearing aids in for them, but they are still unable to hear. The FIRST thing you should do is

   a) ensure the battery compartment is closed.
   b) ask the nurse for new batteries.
   c) inform the nurse that the client's hearing aids do not work.
   d) check to ensure that the volume is turned up.

6. When using a disposable razor to shave a client's face, you should shave

   a) downward over all the areas of the face and neck.
   b) downward over the upper lip and chin; upward on the cheek and neck.
   c) downward over the cheeks, upper lip, and chin; upward on the neck.
   d) upward over all areas of the face and neck.

7. The nursing assistant should line the sink with a barrier during denture care in order to

   a) prevent germs from getting on the dentures.
   b) prevent damage to the dentures if they are dropped.
   c) keep the surfaces of the sink clean.
   d) have a clean area to set the dentures down.

8. You need to provide oral care for an unconscious client. You should open their mouth using

   a) your gloved hand.
   b) a premoistened oral swab.
   c) the client's toothbrush.
   d) a gauze-wrapped wooden tongue depressor.

9. Otto is a client who has diabetes. Today is Otto's bath day, and they need to have their nail care done. You should

   a) ask an experienced nursing assistant to trim Otto's nails.
   b) clean, trim, and file Otto's fingernails.
   c) ask the nurse to trim Otto's fingernails.
   d) have the occupational therapist provide nail care.

10. Donald is an older client with dementia. You are assigned to assist Donald with their nail care but find it difficult to do so because they become upset and lash out. You should

    a) complete Donald's nail care while they are sleeping.
    b) ask another nursing assistant to complete it for you.
    c) use a wrist restraint to hold Donald's hand down while you do their nail care.
    d) skip the nail care, since it is upsetting to the client.

11. When using an electric razor with three rotating heads, you should shave the client's face

    a) in the direction of the hair growth.
    b) against the direction of hair growth.
    c) in small, rotating circles.
    d) in large circles until smooth.

20.E Choose the best response to the following scenarios.

1. Your male client has asked you to help them apply their makeup. What should you do?

   a) Tell them that it is not appropriate.
   b) Help them apply the makeup.
   c) Update their family regarding the request.
   d) Suggest that they not put makeup on today.

2. You are assigned to care for two clients who reside in the same room. Both clients are named Mary, wear glasses, and suffer from dementia. You are unsure whose glasses belong to whom. What should you do?

   a) Guess whose glasses belong to whom.
   b) Ask the clients to identify their glasses.
   c) Ask the nurse to identify the glasses.
   d) Call each client's family to describe the glasses.

3. Your client's family has provided them with a package of razors and requests that you help them shave. What should you do?

   a) Promptly help them shave and keep the package of razors in their room for the next time.
   b) Take the razors away from them; these are not allowed in long-term care facilities.
   c) Ask the client to shave themselves, as you are not trained to do so.
   d) Verify with the care plan that they can use disposable razors.

4. Your client is unconscious. What should you use to provide oral care?

   a) a hard-bristled toothbrush
   b) a soft-bristled toothbrush
   c) an oral swab
   d) Do not provide oral care; they are a choking risk.

5. Your client asks you to apply lotion between their toes after foot care. What should you do?

   a) Apply lotion between their toes as requested.
   b) Explain that it is not within your scope of practice.
   c) Ask the nurse for baby powder to use instead of lotion.
   d) Report the client's request to the nurse and ask for directives.

6. You find your client sobbing because of their hair loss due to cancer treatments. What should you do?

   a) Tell them that you understand and move on to the next task.
   b) Suggest that they purchase a wig or scarf to cover their head.
   c) Allow the client to express their feelings and then report this to the nurse.
   d) Tell them that it is not that bad; there are many people who are bald.

Name _____

Chapter 21: Nutrition

21.A Matching Definitions

_____ 1. Malnutrition
_____ 2. Blood glucose
_____ 3. Dehydration
_____ 4. Total parenteral nutrition
_____ 5. Hypervitaminosis
_____ 6. Calorie
_____ 7. Lipids
_____ 8. Lactase
_____ 9. Lactose
_____ 10. Enteral feeding

A. The enzyme that breaks down lactose
B. The energy the body needs to perform life functions within all its different cells
C. Occurs when the body takes in less fluid than it excretes
D. A unit of measurement; measures food energy
E. A high level of vitamins in the body causing toxic symptoms
F. The sugar found in milk and some dairy products
G. A fluid filled with all the vitamins and minerals a person needs, usually including lipids
H. Fat molecules needed by the body to make use of fat-soluble vitamins; usually given along with TPN
I. A means by which nutrients in a special formula are transported directly into the stomach via a surgically implanted tube
J. Occurs when the body does not receive the nutrients or calories needed

21.B Reflective Short-Answer Exercises

Oliver has diabetes. Oliver was admitted for uncontrolled blood sugar levels to the long-term care facility where you work. Oliver also has open sores on their feet, heart disease, and high cholesterol. Tonight, Oliver refuses their supper tray, stating that they are going to eat pepperoni pizza and soda instead.

1. Is it Oliver's right to eat poorly? Why or why not?

_____
_____
_____
_____

2. How can you encourage Oliver to make good food choices?

_____
_____
_____
_____

Name _____

3. What if Oliver continues to make food choices that are not good for them?
   _____
   _____
   _____
   _____

4. What types of carbohydrates will Oliver be ingesting with their choice of supper?
   _____
   _____
   _____
   _____

5. What types of fat do you think would be part of Oliver's chosen supper?
   _____
   _____
   _____
   _____

6. How might eating these types of fat affect their health?
   _____
   _____
   _____
   _____

7. What foods would be a protein source in Oliver's chosen meal?
   _____
   _____
   _____
   _____

8. Would this be a good protein source? Why or why not?
   _____
   _____
   _____
   _____

9. What diet—or diets—might Oliver benefit from? Why?
   _____
   _____
   _____
   _____

Name _____

21.C Fill in the blanks using terms found in the word bank.

dairy	hypervitaminosis	vegetables
water-soluble	encourages	starches
enzyme	calories	dialysis
grains	MyPlate	blood sugar

1. _____ provides the energy our body needs to perform life functions within all its different cells.
2. Food energy is measured in _____.
3. Adults should get at least 2–3 cups of _____ each day.
4. _____ is a high level of vitamins in the body that causes toxic symptoms.
5. Lactase is the _____ that breaks down lactose.
6. Lactose is the sugar found in milk and some _____ products.
7. Healthy eating _____ healthy lifestyles.
8. _____ is an online tool that can help you choose the right types and amounts of foods to eat each day.
9. The basic forms of carbohydrates are sugars, _____, and fiber.
10. There are two different types of vitamins: fat-soluble and _____.
11. Sometimes clients receiving _____ treatments may have only ice chips in place of water.
12. On average, adults should get about six to eight servings of _____ per day.

21.D Multiple-Choice Exercises

1. MyPlate can assist you in making good food choices by helping to
   a) identify which foods should be increased.
   b) determine which foods should be decreased.
   c) focus on balancing calories.
   d) do all of the above.

2. A good source of complex carbohydrates would be
   a) honey.
   b) pork chops.
   c) black beans.
   d) corn syrup.

3. The body uses calcium for
   a) reducing inflammation.
   b) bone growth.
   c) wound healing.
   d) vision health.

4. You need to document how much fluid Gloria drank for breakfast. Gloria had one 8-ounce glass of milk and one 4-ounce glass of orange juice. How many cc did Gloria drink?
   a) 12 cc
   b) 240 cc
   c) 360 cc
   d) 30 cc

Name _____

5. All of the following are counted toward a client's fluid intake EXCEPT

   a) regular coffee.
   b) Popsicles.
   c) ice cream.
   d) milk.

6. The recommended amount of grain for an average adult is

   a) 3–4 servings each day.
   b) 6–8 servings each day.
   c) 8–10 servings each day.
   d) none of the above.

7. The lunch menu for today includes split pea soup. What food group does the soup belong to?

   a) proteins
   b) vegetables
   c) grains
   d) both a and b

8. A client that is on a low-sodium diet should avoid eating

   a) brown rice.
   b) legumes.
   c) cottage cheese.
   d) spinach.

9. Your responsibilities when caring for a client with diabetes include

   a) ensuring that the nurse has checked the client's blood sugar before meals.
   b) informing the client that they must follow their diabetic diet.
   c) teaching the client what foods are included in a diabetic diet.
   d) telling their family that they should not bring home-cooked foods to the client.

10. Micah is on a lactose-free diet. Today's lunch menu includes ice cream for dessert. The person responsible for ensuring that Micah is not accidentally served ice cream is the

    a) nurse.
    b) nursing assistant.
    c) dietitian.
    d) doctor.

11. Dehydration can be a result of

    a) nausea and vomiting.
    b) diarrhea.
    c) poor fluid intake.
    d) all of the above.

12. A client with celiac disease should avoid eating

    a) most grains.
    b) fruits and vegetables.
    c) dairy products.
    d) meats high in fat.

13. Amanda is a 60-year-old client recovering from a recent car accident. They have a broken right arm and hand. An appropriate diet for Amanda might be a(n)

    a) pureed diet.
    b) enteral feeding.
    c) cut-up diet.
    d) ground diet.

14. You discover that one of your clients with diabetes has been keeping chocolate candy in their room. You should

    a) take the candy out of the room.
    b) inform the client that they should not eat candy.
    c) leave the candy where you found it and update the nurse.
    d) replace the chocolate with sugar-free candy.

15. Before meals, you should make sure all clients have

    a) clean hands.
    b) a clothing protector on.
    c) their food cut up.
    d) salt and pepper to season their food.

Name _____

21.E Choose the best response to the following scenarios.

1. Your client is on a fluid restriction and asks you to fill their water pitcher above the allowed amount. What should you do?

   a) Fill the pitcher as per the client request.
   b) Fill the water pitcher with more ice.
   c) Remind the client of their fluid restriction and update the nurse.
   d) Refuse to give them the requested amount.

2. Alma is an older client with dementia. You notice that Alma eats more at mealtime when they can pick things up with their fingers. What should you do?

   a) Continue trying to persuade Alma to eat with the utensils.
   b) Make sure that Alma is wearing a clothing protector around their neck and across their lap at all times.
   c) Update the nurse and ask if finger foods can be incorporated into Alma's meals.
   d) Make sure that Alma has soft foods for every meal.

3. One of your clients refuses to follow a well-balanced diet and keeps many unhealthy snacks in their room. What should you do?

   a) Take the snacks away when they are napping.
   b) Tell the family to remove the snacks and not to bring more.
   c) Remove the snacks and then place them at the nurse's station.
   d) Update the nurse so that they can reinforce diet recommendations with them.

4. You find your client taking multiple vitamins brought from home while eating their breakfast. What should you do?

   a) Update the nurse right away.
   b) Ask them to give them to you.
   c) Tell the family that they need to take them home.
   d) Offer to put them in the locked drawer of their bedside table.

5. Your client has chosen to eat their breakfast in their room. You have their breakfast tray and are about to place it on the bedside table when you notice a full urinal on the table. What should you do?

   a) Place the food tray next to the full urinal and then empty the urinal.
   b) Empty the urinal, sanitize the bedside table, and then place their food on the bedside table.
   c) Place the urinal on top of the dresser next to them and then place their food on the bedside table.
   d) Ask the client to eat in the dining room while you tidy their bedroom.

6. Your client receives a mechanically altered diet and asks you what the green food is. What should you do?

   a) Tell them that you have no idea.
   b) Taste the food and offer an idea.
   c) Smell the food and offer an idea.
   d) Look at the day's menu and update the client.

7. While feeding one of your clients with dementia, they become agitated and spit food in your hair. What should you do?

   a) Firmly tell them that it is wrong to spit foods.
   b) Excuse yourself, clean up, and report the behavior to the nurse.
   c) Refuse to feed them the rest of the meal.
   d) Laugh it off; they don't know what they're doing.

8. Your client vomits during dinner. What would you do?

   a) Clean the client and then ask if they would like to eat the rest of their meal in their room.
   b) Take the client to their room where you can care for them and then update the nurse.
   c) Offer another food choice like chicken noodle soup or gelatin.
   d) Clean the client and then take them to their room for a nap.

Chapter 21 • 103

This page intentionally left blank.

Chapter 22: Elimination and Specimen Collection

22.A Matching Definitions

_____ 1. Occult blood
_____ 2. Colostomy
_____ 3. Urostomy
_____ 4. Urinary retention
_____ 5. Frank blood
_____ 6. Urinary analysis
_____ 7. Ileostomy
_____ 8. Suppository
_____ 9. Suprapubic catheter
_____ 10. Stoma

A. Red, obvious blood

B. A catheter that is inserted through a surgical opening in the abdomen and directly into the bladder

C. One end of the large intestine is drawn outside of the abdominal wall for the passage of stool

D. A wax cone that is inserted into the rectum to aid in a bowel movement

E. The inability to partially, or completely, empty the bladder

F. Hidden blood

G. One end of the small intestine is drawn outside of the abdominal wall for the passage of stool

H. A test that looks for bacteria in the urine

I. The ureters are detached from the bladder and then attached to a segment of bowel, one end of which extends outside of the abdominal wall, allowing urine to drain to the outside of the body

J. An opening that protrudes from the abdomen connecting an internal organ to the outside of the body

22.B Reflective Short-Answer Exercises

Mario is a 29-year-old quadriplegic. You help Mario in their home 4 days a week with bathing and range-of-motion exercises. When you are not there, Mario's mother helps care for them. Mario has an indwelling catheter and a colostomy, which they find embarrassing. Today you find that the area around the catheter is bleeding.

1. Is Mario at high risk for skin breakdown? Why or why not?

_____
_____
_____
_____

Name _____

2. Why do you think Mario needs an indwelling catheter?

   _____
   _____
   _____
   _____

3. Where would you attach Mario's catheter holder?

   _____
   _____
   _____
   _____

4. If a catheter holder were not available, what would you do?

   _____
   _____
   _____
   _____

5. What supplies would Mario need at home so that you are able to empty the collection bag and measure their urine output appropriately?

   _____
   _____
   _____
   _____

6. If a bowel movement occurs via the colostomy, would you still document it? Why or why not?

   _____
   _____
   _____
   _____

22.C Fill in the blanks using terms found in the word bank.

abdomen	elimination	hidden
bedpan	bladder	urinary retention
incontinence garment	suppository	colostomy
indwelling catheter	catheter holder	hemorrhoids
contamination		

1. A(n) _____ is when one end of the large intestine is drawn outside of the abdominal wall for the passage of stool.
2. A(n) _____ is a wax cone that is inserted into the rectum to aid in a bowel movement.
3. _____ are large distended veins found in and around the anus.
4. A suprapubic catheter is a catheter that is inserted through an opening in the abdomen directly into the _____.

Name _____

5. To avoid _____ while collecting the urine for a UA, first clean the client's peri-area.

6. _____ is the inability to partially, or totally, empty the bladder.

7. Assisting clients with _____ needs, such as toileting and changing incontinence products, is a large part of the nursing assistant role.

8. If a client is totally dependent on you for elimination needs, you will have to change their _____ every 2 hours.

9. Occult blood is _____ blood.

10. A stoma is an opening that protrudes from the _____ and connects an internal organ to the outside of the body.

11. Some clients may require a(n) _____, which stays in the bladder for a long period of time.

12. A(n) _____ is a device used to decrease the amount of pulling on the catheter and thus trauma to the urethra and bladder.

13. Never obtain a clean catch urine sample from a _____, urinal, or commode because it will alter the results of the urinalysis.

22.D Multiple-Choice Exercises

1. A client who is incontinent should be assisted to the toilet
   a) twice in an 8-hour shift.
   b) once in the morning and once in the evening.
   c) every 2 hours.
   d) every hour while awake.

2. Bernard is an older client who is at risk of falling due to poor mobility and dementia. While Bernard is sitting on the toilet, you should
   a) make Bernard's bed and tidy up the room.
   b) tell Bernard to call for assistance when ready.
   c) ask Bernard if they wish you to give them privacy.
   d) remain in the bathroom with Bernard.

3. An indwelling catheter should be cleaned by
   a) moving the washcloth up and down the catheter until clean.
   b) starting closest to the body and moving downward about 4 inches.
   c) starting farthest from the body and moving upward about 4 inches.
   d) starting closest to the body and moving downward about 8 inches.

4. Before receiving an enema, a client should be
   a) lying on their right side in bed.
   b) sitting on a toilet or commode.
   c) lying on their left side in bed.
   d) lying on their back with the head of the bed up.

5. Doreen is a client who is given an oral laxative for constipation. If Doreen is unable to have a bowel movement after taking the laxative, the nurse is likely to administer a(n)
   a) soap suds enema.
   b) over-the-counter enema.
   c) suppository.
   d) liquid stool softener.

6. Urinary retention may be caused by
   a) the brain not being able to send messages to the body.
   b) the body not being able to receive messages from the brain.
   c) a blockage in the urinary tract.
   d) all of the above.

Name _____

7. Elmer is a client recovering from a hip replacement. Elmer tells you that they need to use the bathroom to have a bowel movement. Elmer's care plan states that they are an assist of two for transfers, but you are unable to find a coworker to help you. You should

   a) offer Elmer a fracture pan.
   b) offer Elmer a traditional bed pan.
   c) ask Elmer if they can wait until you find help.
   d) offer to help Elmer use a bedside commode.

8. When emptying a colostomy bag, the nursing assistant should clean the skin around the stoma with

   a) damp paper towels.
   b) alcohol wipes.
   c) adult wipes.
   d) ostomy powder.

9. The FIRST step in collecting a urine sample is to

   a) assist the client to the toilet.
   b) label the specimen container.
   c) put on your gown and gloves.
   d) assemble your supplies.

10. Clara is a client who is incontinent. While bathing Clara this morning, you notice a dime-sized open area on one of their buttocks. You should

    a) clean the area with adult wipes and apply barrier cream.
    b) make sure that Clara is covered and safe, and then ask the nurse to look at the area.
    c) get Clara dressed and then tell the nurse about the open area.
    d) sprinkle powder in the clean brief to absorb moisture.

11. Urine specimens may be collected to

    a) check for sugar levels.
    b) determine kidney function.
    c) measure potassium levels.
    d) do all of the above.

12. When collecting a stool sample, the nursing assistant should make sure that the sample is

    a) taken from a new commode or bedpan.
    b) not contaminated with toilet paper.
    c) not contaminated with urine.
    d) all of the above.

13. You have been assigned to obtain a stool specimen from one of your clients. After they have a bowel movement, you should take a sample from

    a) both ends and the middle of the stool.
    b) the middle of the stool only.
    c) both ends of the stool only.
    d) one end of the stool only.

22.E Choose the best response to the following scenarios.

1. While changing your client's colostomy bag, you become nauseated from the smell. What should you do?

   a) Tell the client you are becoming ill.
   b) Refuse to change the ostomy bag next time.
   c) Do your best to finish the task in a professional manner.
   d) Ask another nursing assistant to complete the task.

2. Your client complains of pain at the catheter insertion site. What should you do?

   a) Deflate the balloon and reposition the tube.
   b) Put analgesic cream around the tube.
   c) Ask the nurse to remove the catheter.
   d) Report the complaints of pain to the nurse.

Name _____

3. Your client who is normally continent has had a bowel movement in their bed and is very embarrassed. What should you do?

   a) Place an incontinence garment on them to prevent more accidents.
   b) Call their family and ask that they bring in incontinence products for them.
   c) Clean them in a caring and professional manner and place clean linens on their bed.
   d) Put them on the commode every 2 hours for the rest of your shift.

4. You work at an assisted-living facility. This morning you used the last of a client's incontinence briefs. What should you do?

   a) Use towels in place of the incontinence product; the family does not have much money.
   b) Ask the nurse to contact the family and request more be brought in right away.
   c) Borrow briefs from the roommate if they use similar incontinence products.
   d) Ask the nurse to insert a catheter until the family can bring in more briefs.

5. Your client requests their colostomy bag be changed, and their roommate is having breakfast on the other side of the room. What would you do?

   a) Change the bag as the client requests.
   b) Tell the client to wait until the roommate is finished with breakfast.
   c) Take the client to another restroom and change the bag.
   d) Take the breakfast away from the roommate while you change the bag.

6. Your client has had five large loose bowel movements during your shift. What should you do?

   a) Only use hand sanitizer when caring for this client.
   b) Report the loose stools to the nurse and follow their directives.
   c) Return home to change your uniform.
   d) Obtain a stool specimen to check for possible illness.

This page intentionally left blank.

Name _____

Chapter 23: Care for the Client with Dementia and Cognitive or Mental Health Challenges

23.A Matching Definitions

_____ 1. Sundowning

_____ 2. Dementia

_____ 3. Elope

A. A general term describing loss of brain function and memory

B. An increase in agitation and restlessness later in the day and into the evening

C. Leaving the home or facility unsupervised

23.B Reflective Short-Answer Exercises

Olga is a 68-year-old client with Alzheimer's disease. Olga's partner Harry can no longer care for Olga at home. Harry is unable to rest or get sleep because Olga is up all night wandering around the house. Olga is moving to the nursing home today. Olga seems anxious and is rummaging through their dresser when you enter the room. When you try to talk to Olga, they don't look at you or answer. When you approach, they begin screaming and push you away. Harry is upset and questions if placing Olga in a nursing home was the right decision.

1. Can Olga recover from this disease?

   _____
   _____
   _____
   _____

2. What stage of dementia do you think Olga is in right now?

   _____
   _____
   _____
   _____

3. What are some common symptoms of dementia that Olga is displaying in this scenario?

   _____
   _____
   _____
   _____

4. What unmet needs might Olga have that would make them lash out?

   _____
   _____
   _____
   _____

Name _____

5. What therapeutic interventions might help Olga in this scenario?
   _____
   _____
   _____

6. What should your demeanor be when approaching Olga?
   _____
   _____
   _____
   _____

7. How can you keep Olga safe when they wake up at night?
   _____
   _____
   _____

8. What can help Olga be safe in regard to them wandering while in the facility?
   _____
   _____
   _____
   _____

9. Why do you think Harry is so upset? Why do they doubt their decision to put Olga in the nursing home?
   _____
   _____
   _____
   _____

23.C Fill in the blanks using terms found in the word bank.

managed	memory	intellectual disability
unmet	sexual	restlessness
Alzheimer's	mental illness	plaques
obsessed	dementia	behaviors
memories	elopement	tangles

1. Dementia is a general term describing loss of _____ and brain function.
2. _____ is a cognitively challenged client leaving the facility or home without supervision.
3. Sundowning is the increase in _____ and agitation later in the day and into the evening.

112 • Chapter 23

Name _____

4. The most common type of dementia is _____.

5. Alzheimer's disease is characterized by _____ and _____ that form in the brain.

6. Alzheimer's _____ can be divided into three stages.

7. Certain _____, such as impaired communication, wandering, and difficulty performing activities of daily living, are commonly seen in people with dementia.

8. A(n) _____ means that the client will have problems with thinking and learning.

9. Clients may display behaviors associated with dementia because of a(n) _____ need.

10. Clients with dementia may become _____ with leaving a facility to get home, and it is difficult to redirect them.

11. _____ inappropriateness may occur in the later stages of dementia, which can be quite upsetting to both the family of the client and others residing in the facility.

12. Reminiscence therapy is used to help the client recall distant _____ of their life.

13. The behaviors associated with dementia can be _____ by going through a checklist of common triggers or unmet needs.

14. _____ occurs when there is a concern with mood, behavior, and/or thinking.

23.D Multiple-Choice Exercises

1. Plaques and tangles in the brain are characteristic of
   a) Lewy body dementia.
   b) vascular dementia.
   c) Parkinson's disease.
   d) Alzheimer's disease.

2. Anna is a client who is in the early stage of dementia. Anna is on medication for Alzheimer's disease. These medications can help Anna by
   a) reversing the effects of Alzheimer's.
   b) slowing the progression of dementia.
   c) stopping the disease from progressing.
   d) providing a cure for Alzheimer's.

3. Theresa is a 78-year-old client with Alzheimer's. Theresa is often restless and anxious, especially in the evenings. You can help reduce Theresa's anxiety by
   a) looking at a photo album together.
   b) giving Theresa some clean towels to fold.
   c) turning on the TV for Theresa.
   d) doing both a and b.

4. One of the first symptoms of dementia is
   a) the inability to hold a conversation with others.
   b) difficulty swallowing foods.
   c) short-term memory loss.
   d) sexual inappropriateness.

5. A diagnosis of Alzheimer's disease is made by the doctor based on
   a) laboratory tests.
   b) mental and physical examinations.
   c) the client's signs and symptoms.
   d) all of the above.

6. Estelle is an older adult client with dementia. This afternoon you find Estelle by the nurse's desk pacing back and forth, visibly upset. The first thing you should do for Estelle is to
   a) assist Estelle to the bathroom and ensure that they are dry and comfortable.
   b) encourage Estelle to visit another client in the facility.
   c) give Estelle an art project to work on in their room.
   d) tell the nurse that Estelle needs medication for anxiety.

7. Alberto is a client with late-stage Alzheimer's. Alberto is no longer able to speak or follow directives. An appropriate activity for Alberto would be

   a) bingo.
   b) arts and crafts.
   c) morning exercise group.
   d) an ice cream social.

8. You work in a long-term care facility that has a unit designed for clients with dementia. Today you have noticed that one of your coworkers has been very impatient and short-tempered with their clients. You should

   a) tell your coworker that you will cover for them while they take their cigarette break.
   b) ignore it; all caregivers have difficult days.
   c) report your observations to the nurse right away.
   d) suggest to the coworker that they take some time off from work.

9. Charlotte is an older adult client with Alzheimer's disease. Charlotte's partner, Arnie, has been taking care of Charlotte at home for all of their daily care. Arnie is exhausted but does not want to admit Charlotte to a facility. Respite options for Arnie may include

   a) an adult day care service.
   b) a limited stay at a hospital.
   c) a home health aide.
   d) both a and c.

10. Doreen is a client with moderate dementia. At supper, you notice that Doreen has had a large, loose incontinent stool. When you attempt to toilet and change Doreen, they become upset and starts yelling at you. You should

    a) continue attempting to toilet and clean Doreen.
    b) let Doreen rest for a few minutes and then reapproach them.
    c) wait until Doreen is ready to go to bed to clean them.
    d) tell Doreen that they have to be washed or their skin will break down.

11. You are caring for a client with dementia who often refuses to have their incontinence garment changed. The most effective phrase to use when assisting them to the bathroom is

    a) "Let's go to the toilet."
    b) "It's time to change your brief."
    c) "Let's just freshen up a bit."
    d) "I'm going to take you to the bathroom now."

12. Tonight one of your clients with dementia has been very wakeful. They have attempted to get out of bed unassisted a number of times. To help your client sleep better at night, you should

    a) keep the unit as quiet and calm as possible.
    b) move them to a room next to the nurse's station.
    c) keep them awake until at least 10:00 p.m.
    d) ask the nurse if they can give the client a sleeping pill.

Name _____

23.E Choose the best response to the following scenarios.

1. While you are bathing a client with dementia, they start to yell and scream. What should you do?

    a) Ignore their yelling; they do this all the time.
    b) Proceed with the bath as quickly as possible.
    c) Do your best to stay calm and keep the client safe.
    d) Leave them alone until they are calm.

2. Two clients who both have dementia are fighting in the hallway. What should you do?

    a) Get their attention by yelling, "Stop," and then separate them.
    b) Talk in a soft tone while separating them.
    c) Explain resident rights to both clients.
    d) Keep calm and call 911.

3. A client whom you are caring for has Alzheimer's. They tell you they are waiting for their husband to visit. You know that their husband has been dead for 20 years. What should you do?

    a) Tell them that you will let them know if you see their husband and redirect them to another activity.
    b) Tell them that their husband will not be coming to see them.
    c) Ask the nurse to give them some medicine to calm their nerves.
    d) Remind them that their husband passed away some time ago and then offer to take them to activities.

4. You are caring for a client who has middle stage Alzheimer's disease. You find them dressed in their best clothing. They tell you that they are going out to church. What should you do?

    a) Offer to take them to church when you are done with your shift.
    b) Offer them a visit from the resident chaplain.
    c) Arrange a taxi for their ride and call the church so that they can be prepared for them.
    d) Tell them that they cannot go to church and change them into more appropriate clothing for the day.

5. You are caring for a client with dementia. They seem restless and agitated after lunch. What intervention should you try?

    a) Leave them alone to decrease stimulus.
    b) Separate them from the group so they do not pick a fight.
    c) Turn on the TV in their room to distract them.
    d) Take them to the bathroom.

6. You are caring for a client who has dementia. They take their pants off in the dining room during supper. What should you do?

    a) Remove the other clients from the area, and then pull up their pants so they can resume eating.
    b) Walk them back to their room with their pants off and then toilet them.
    c) Help them pull up their pants and then assist them to the bathroom.
    d) After pulling up their pants, put a belt on them so that they cannot take off their pants by themself.

7. You are caring for a client with Alzheimer's. They are crying and holding their head. What is the first thing you should do?

    a) Get them some pain medication.
    b) Rub their back to try to soothe them.
    c) Remove them from the area.
    d) Take them to play bingo.

This page intentionally left blank.

Name _____

Chapter 24: Oxygen Therapy and Respiratory Interventions

24.A Matching Definitions

_____ 1. Incentive spirometer

_____ 2. Acute condition

_____ 3. Chronic condition

A. A disease, illness, or injury that lasts for a long period of time

B. A medical device used to maintain lung function, or as an aid during respiratory illness

C. A short-lived new injury or illness, which may or may not be resolved

24.B Reflective Short Answer Exercises

AJ is a client who had a fall a week ago and is now staying in bed more often and refusing to participate in activities. Today AJ is coughing, has a fever, and is found to have pneumonia.

1. Does AJ have an acute or chronic respiratory illness?

   _____
   _____
   _____
   _____

2. Why do you think AJ developed pneumonia?

   _____
   _____
   _____
   _____

3. AJ now has an order for oxygen via nasal cannula at 2 liters per minute. The nurse brings an oxygen concentrator to AJ's room and turns it on to 2 liters per minute. What additional nursing assistant responsibilities do you have now that AJ has oxygen?

   _____
   _____
   _____
   _____

4. What would be the nursing assistant's responsibilities in regard to oxygen use if AJ must leave the facility for a doctor's appointment?

   _____
   _____
   _____
   _____

Name _____

5. How would you maintain the oxygen concentrator in AJ's room to ensure that it is working properly?

_____
_____
_____
_____

6. What can you do to help ease any anxiety AJ may experience due to shortness of breath from the pneumonia?

_____
_____
_____
_____

7. What two exercises may be ordered to help resolve AJ's pneumonia?

_____
_____
_____
_____

8. What are the nursing assistant's responsibilities in regard to these exercises?

_____
_____
_____
_____

24.C Fill in the blanks using terms found in the word bank.

cylinders	deep breathing	face mask
acute condition	oxygen	long
nasal cannula	continuous	incentive spirometer
anxious	drug	physician

1. A(n) _____ is a short-lived new illness or injury, which may or may not be resolved.
2. A chronic condition is a disease, injury, or illness that lasts for a _____ period of time.
3. A(n) _____ is a medical device used to maintain lung function in chronic illness or used as an aid during an acute respiratory illness.
4. Clients may require _____ for chronic or acute respiratory conditions.
5. Oxygen is a(n) _____ and therefore cannot be legally administered by the nursing assistant.
6. A(n) _____ is a long plastic tube with nasal prongs at the end of it, which delivers low doses of oxygen to the client.
7. Your client may become _____ or irritable when they are having difficulty breathing.

8. Coughing and _____ exercises can help maintain the client's lung function by expanding the lung tissue and clearing the lungs of mucus.

9. Oxygen is delivered when ordered by the _____. It is used for chronic or acute respiratory conditions.

10. A(n) _____ can be used to deliver higher amounts of concentrated oxygen.

11. One side effect of _____ oxygen usage is nosebleeds.

12. Oxygen can be stored in small and large metal _____.

24.D Multiple Choice Exercises

1. Dory is a client with COPD who requires supplementary oxygen. Today they have been using their call light every 15 minutes for small tasks. You try to tend to Dory's needs, but they just become more anxious. You should

    a) have another nursing assistant take over Dory's care.
    b) take more breaks to reduce stress.
    c) inform the nurse of Dory's anxiety right away.
    d) tell the nurse about Dory's behavior at the end of your shift.

2. An example of a chronic condition would be

    a) influenza.
    b) osteoarthritis.
    c) chicken pox.
    d) the common cold.

3. One of your clients is on oxygen at 2 liters per minute via a nasal cannula. Their oxygen tubing is connected to the concentrator in their room. This afternoon they are asking to go to for a walk. You should

    a) change the client over to a portable tank and check the flow rate.
    b) push the concentrator down the hallway with them.
    c) remove their oxygen while you ambulate them.
    d) ask the nurse to ambulate them.

4. The flow rate for supplementary oxygen is typically

    a) 8–10 liters per minute.
    b) 6–8 liters per minute.
    c) 10–12 liters per minute.
    d) 1–6 liters per minute.

5. Mateo is a client who is on oxygen via a nasal cannula. Today Mateo tells you that their nose is stuffy and dry. You should update the nurse and

    a) place petroleum jelly in Mateo's nostrils.
    b) place distilled water in Mateo's concentrator.
    c) watch for nosebleeds.
    d) both b and c.

6. One of your clients requires oxygen at night while they sleep. When placing the nasal cannula on them, the FIRST step should be

    a) inserting the cannula with the prongs facing the client.
    b) placing the tubing loop over the client's ears.
    c) verifying that the oxygen supply is on.
    d) bringing the sliding connector toward the client's chin.

7. The oxygen delivery system most commonly used in a hospital is a

    a) standard concentrator.
    b) wall-mounted system.
    c) large cylinder with a conventional regulator.
    d) small cylinder with a conserving regulator.

8. You are walking past one of your client's rooms when you hear their oxygen concentrator alarm beeping. You should

   a) ensure that the concentrator's filter is clean.
   b) refill the concentrator with oxygen.
   c) check how much oxygen is in the concentrator.
   d) call the client's oxygen supplier.

9. The most comfortable position for a client on oxygen typically is

   a) supine.
   b) side-lying.
   c) semi-Fowler's.
   d) prone.

10. You can assist a client with maintaining lung function by

    a) reinforcing coughing and deep breathing exercises.
    b) teaching the client how to use an incentive spirometer.
    c) starting the client on oxygen if they become short of breath.
    d) turning up the oxygen flow rate if the client is anxious.

11. You are assigned to care for Leo, a 65-year-old client with pneumonia. The nurse has directed you to assist Leo with their incentive spirometer. You will need to read Leo's care plan to

    a) check if Leo will be using the spirometer when they go home.
    b) verify how often Leo should use the spirometer.
    c) check that Leo has a doctor's order for the spirometer.
    d) get directions on how to use Leo's spirometer.

12. Coughing and deep breathing exercises help the client by

    a) eliminating germs in the lungs.
    b) expanding the lung tissue.
    c) clearing the lungs of mucus.
    d) doing both b and c.

24.E Choose the best response to the following scenarios.

1. Sarena is having difficulty breathing and asks you to turn their oxygen up to 5 liters. What would you do?

   a) Promptly turn the oxygen up to 5 liters for Sarena; this is their right.
   b) Report the shortness of breath to the nurse right away and ask that they assess Sarena.
   c) Report the shortness of breath to the nurse at the end of the shift.
   d) Ask Sarena to turn it up themselves, since this is out of your scope of practice.

2. Your client who has a chronic lung disease is calling you into their room every 10 minutes for a variety of small tasks. What should you do?

   a) Explain to them that you do not have time to keep coming into their room.
   b) Ignore the call light; many other clients need your help too.
   c) Reassure the client and update the nurse.
   d) Take the call light away from the client while caring for your other clients' needs.

Name _____

3. You notice Simone taking off their nasal cannula and not wearing it as prescribed. What should you do?

   a) Ask Simone why they don't use it and then report this to the nurse.
   b) Turn off the oxygen so that it is not wasted.
   c) Tell Simone that they need to wear the oxygen at all times.
   d) Turn down the oxygen's flow rate.

4. Your client is applying Vaseline™ petroleum jelly to their nares due to dryness from oxygen use. What is the BEST response?

   a) Assist them in applying the jelly to prevent more nosebleeds.
   b) Take the petroleum jelly away and give it to the nurse.
   c) Report to the nurse and offer them a water-soluble lubricant.
   d) Tell them to stay away from fire or sparks.

5. Your client is on continuous oxygen. You find them sitting outside smoking a cigarette. What should you do?

   a) Remove all clients from that side of the building.
   b) Take the cigarettes and lighter away from them immediately.
   c) Immediately report this to nurse.
   d) Tell them that they need to take cigarette breaks only when staff is with them.

6. You find an oxygen cylinder sitting upright in a client's room. It is not being used. What should you do?

   a) Leave it there; the client might have to use it later.
   b) Take it to the proper storage area and update the nurse.
   c) Lay it on its side so that it doesn't fall over.
   d) Place it in the client's closet for safekeeping.

This page intentionally left blank.

Chapter 25: Care for the Medical and Surgical Client

25.A Matching Definitions

_____ 1. Splinting

_____ 2. Ambulatory surgery

_____ 3. Atelectasis

A. A respiratory disorder in which gas exchange is limited due to either alveoli collapse or fluid buildup, causing chest pain, coughing, and sometimes respiratory distress

B. A surgical procedure that does not require an overnight stay; also called same-day surgery

C. A process that decreases pain by supporting the chest and abdomen during coughing and deep breathing

25.B Reflective Short Answer Exercises

Loretta is recovering from a car accident and has had multiple surgeries to their chest and abdomen. Loretta has an IV and is NPO. You are responsible for applying sequential stockings and repositioning Loretta every 2 hours.

1. Would Loretta be a medical or a surgical client?

2. Why would Loretta be NPO?

3. When might Loretta advance past NPO status?

4. What is Loretta's activity level at this point?

5. What respiratory complications is Loretta at risk for, and why?

_____
_____
_____
_____

6. What cardiac complications is Loretta at risk for, and why?

_____
_____
_____
_____

7. What will the sequential stockings do for Loretta?

_____
_____
_____
_____

8. What would you have to be aware of when repositioning Loretta?

_____
_____
_____
_____

25.C Fill in the blanks using terms found in the word bank.

doctor	ambulatory surgery	supports
assesses	atelectasis	blood clots
ears	medical	walking
immobility	cardiac	acute care
resist	intravenous	

1. _____ is a respiratory disorder in which gas exchange is limited. It can cause chest pain, coughing, and sometimes respiratory distress.

2. A surgical procedure that does not require an overnight stay is called _____.

3. Splinting is the intervention that _____ the chest and abdomen during coughing and deep breathing to decrease pain.

4. TED hose are tight elastic stockings designed to help prevent _____ from forming in the legs.

5. _____ is a hospital-based healthcare service.

6. You are the eyes and _____ of the nurse.

7. _____ clients are people who have a chronic or acute medical illness that needs to be monitored closely in a hospital setting.

Name _____

8. Activity level for the client is determined by the _____, nurse, and therapy team.

9. _____ is an intervention that can significantly decrease the risk of postsurgical complications.

10. Many times, respiratory complications result from _____ after surgery.

11. _____ complications, such as a blood clot, may also result from the immobility associated with surgery or a medical illness.

12. Many clients in hospitals have continuous _____ (IV) therapy.

13. The nurse continuously _____ the client's tolerance of diet before progressing to the next level.

14. Postsurgical clients may _____ activity because of the pain.

25.D Multiple Choice Exercises

1. Typical nursing assistant responsibilities when caring for medical clients include
   a) drawing a client's blood for lab tests.
   b) taking vital signs every 4 hours.
   c) administering a client's insulin.
   d) inserting a urinary catheter.

2. You are assigned to care for Maria, a medical client who speaks only Spanish. You are not familiar with Spanish, and Maria becomes upset and frustrated when you try to assist them. You should
   a) wait until an interpreter is available, and then provide care.
   b) call a family member to come sit with Maria while you care for them.
   c) use facial expressions and hand gestures while you provide care.
   d) ask another nursing assistant to care for Maria.

3. A client who is scheduled for ambulatory surgery can expect to
   a) be discharged home the same day as the surgery.
   b) remain in the hospital overnight.
   c) be discharged to a nursing home for rehabilitation.
   d) check in to the hospital the night before the surgery.

4. One of your clients has been admitted to the hospital for surgery to correct a bowel obstruction. This is an example of a(n)
   a) outpatient surgery.
   b) inpatient surgery.
   c) ambulatory surgery.
   d) same-day surgery.

5. One common complication of surgery is a(n)
   a) blood clot.
   b) heart attack.
   c) asthmatic attack.
   d) stroke.

6. Elsa is a client who had surgery on their left shoulder this morning. Elsa tells you that they are thirsty and would like something to drink. You should
   a) offer Elsa apple juice.
   b) offer Elsa a glass of water.
   c) check Elsa's care plan for their current dietary status.
   d) tell Elsa that they are unable to drink anything.

Name _____

7. Jonathan is a postsurgical client who is on a full-liquid diet. When you enter their room, they are drinking some orange juice. Jonathan tells you that they "feel like throwing up." You should

   a) inform the nurse that Jonathan drank orange juice and is now feeling nauseous.
   b) offer Jonathon something else to drink like white soda or apple juice.
   c) explain that nausea is common after surgery and that it will pass.
   d) offer Jonathan soda crackers and tell them that this will calm their stomach.

8. The weight-bearing status of a surgical client is determined by the client's

   a) nurse.
   b) surgeon.
   c) physical therapist.
   d) occupational therapist.

9. A respiratory disorder in which gas exchange is limited because of alveoli collapse or fluid buildup is called

   a) asthma.
   b) influenza.
   c) tuberculosis.
   d) atelectasis.

10. Jayleen is recovering from right knee replacement surgery. The care plan states that their status is 25% weight bearing. This means that Jayleen can

    a) put 75% of their weight on their right leg.
    b) put 25% of their weight on their right leg.
    c) only toe touch on the right side.
    d) put weight on their right leg as tolerated.

11. Teaching a client how to use an incentive spirometer is the responsibility of

    a) the nurse.
    b) the surgeon.
    c) the respiratory therapist.
    d) either a or c.

12. Edna is a client who had heart surgery 2 days ago. Edna has been taught how to do cough and deep breathing exercises by the nurse, but Edna tells you they don't want to do them because they are afraid that it will hurt. You should

    a) tell Edna that they can use an incentive spirometer instead.
    b) suggest that Edna wait a few more days before starting the exercises.
    c) encourage Edna to splint while performing the exercises.
    d) report Edna's refusal to the respiratory therapist.

13. The BEST time to put a client's TED hose on is

    a) before they get out of bed.
    b) when they are sitting in their chair.
    c) right after their shower.
    d) when they go to bed at night.

14. Joseph is a surgical client who is on strict bed rest. The intervention most likely to be used for preventing blood clots for Joseph is

    a) TED hose.
    b) sequential stockings.
    c) massage therapy.
    d) anti-embolism stockings.

15. You are assigned to care for a surgical patient who has an IV in their left hand. They have asked to wear their own gown. You should

    a) bring the IV bag through the left sleeve first, followed by the left arm.
    b) bring their right arm through the right sleeve first, followed by the left.
    c) bring their left arm through the sleeve first, followed by the IV bag.
    d) suggest that they wear a hospital gown with snaps instead.

16. When placing sequential stockings under a client's leg, you should make sure that

    a) the vinyl side of the stocking is against the client's skin.
    b) you are able to slide four fingers between the stocking and leg.
    c) the cotton side of the stocking is against the client's skin.
    d) you fasten the Velcro® of the stocking starting at the thigh.

Name _____

25.E Choose the best response to the following scenarios.

1. Your client's IV alarm is beeping. What should you do?

    a) Shut it off, and then go report it to the nurse.
    b) Ensure that the client is safe, and then go report to the nurse.
    c) Inform the client that the nurse will be checking the IV soon.
    d) Place the pump on hold, and then go report it to the nurse.

2. Melany refuses to wear their TED hose. What should you do?

    a) Ask Melany why they don't want to wear their TEDs, and then report to the nurse.
    b) It is Melany's right to refuse; do not put them on.
    c) Reapproach Melany the next morning.
    d) Explain the danger of blood clots after surgery to Melany.

3. Luis had surgery yesterday and is doing well. The doctor has written the order to advance the diet as tolerated. Luis tells you they are starving and want to order a pizza. What would you do?

    a) Check Luis' care plan to determine their current diet.
    b) Order Luis a pizza from the hospital kitchen.
    c) Encourage Luis' family to bring in a pizza for them.
    d) Tell Luis that they should not eat for 24 hours.

4. Your client who just had a hip replacement requests to use the restroom. What should you do?

    a) Ambulate the client to the restroom.
    b) Put them on a bedpan until you find the nurse.
    c) Put an incontinent garment on them.
    d) Check the care plan for weight-bearing instructions.

5. Oscar requests a cup of coffee, but you become busy and forget to get them the coffee. The next time you enter the room, Oscar is upset. What should you do?

    a) Apologize and explain that another client needed you more.
    b) Empower Oscar to walk to the kitchenette for a cup of coffee.
    c) Apologize and promptly return with the coffee.
    d) Get a pot of coffee from the kitchen for Oscar to have at their bedside.

6. Your client is complaining of pain and refuses to walk. What should you do?

    a) Encourage the client to walk small amounts.
    b) Tell them that their wife will be upset with them if they don't walk.
    c) Ask the client to do leg exercises in bed instead.
    d) Let the client stay in bed since it is their right.

7. Your surgical client is very tired but continuously has a room full of visitors who are making a lot of noise. What should you do?

    a) Do nothing; they have the right to visit.
    b) Ask the visitors to allow the client to rest.
    c) Tell the visitors to go home and return later.
    d) Wait for them to leave, and then care for the client.

This page intentionally left blank.

Name _____

Chapter 26: End-of-Life Care

26.A Definitions

In your own words, write a definition for the following terms.

1. Mottling:

2. Cheyne-Stokes breathing:

26.B Reflective Short-Answer Exercises

Darshan is an older client who is dying of prostate cancer. Darshan is a practicing Hindu and has pictures of Hindu gods on their bedside table. Darshan's family has been chanting mantras at Darshan's bedside for the last 2 days. Today Darshan is in a coma. Darshan has not voided for the last 24 hours. They have not had a bowel movement for the last 5 days. Darshan can no longer take in anything by mouth. You notice that Darshan has started Cheyne-Stokes breathing, and their lower legs are purple in color.

1. How would you perform your job with Darshan's family present around the clock?

2. What respiratory changes is Darshan going through that tell you they are close to death? How could you explain this to the family?

3. Do you think Darshan can hear the chanting? Why or why not?

4. Do you think the chanting might bring them comfort?

Chapter 26 • 129

Name _____

5. Is it normal for Darshan to not have had a bowel movement for 5 days? Why or why not?

   _____
   _____
   _____

6. Is it normal that Darshan has not voided for a whole day? Why or why not?

   _____
   _____
   _____

7. How can you help Darshan stay comfortable now that they are exhibiting the Cheyne-Stokes breathing pattern?

   _____
   _____
   _____

8. Should you accommodate the family's round-the-clock vigil in Darshan's room?

   _____
   _____
   _____

26.C Fill in the blanks using terms found in the word bank.

decrease	apnea	doctor
mottling	death	hearing
religion	honored	cardiovascular
physical		

1. Cheyne-Stokes breathing is a pattern of fast, shallow breathing followed by slow, deep breathing, with periods of _____.

2. _____ is the appearance of purplish marbling on the skin as a result of poor blood flow to the extremities.

3. People who die from chronic conditions may go through a series of _____ changes such as mottling, dusky nail beds, and respiratory changes.

4. _____ is a part of life.

5. You should feel _____ to help your client and their loved ones through the life event of passing away.

6. As the dying process continues, the _____ system slows down, often resulting in mottling.

7. _____ is the last of the senses to fade.

Name _____

8. As the body begins to slow, appetite and thirst _____, which can frighten family members when the client stops eating and drinking.

9. You cannot assume that everyone is the same _____ or has the same beliefs as you do.

10. The _____ pronounces the client deceased.

26.D Multiple-Choice Exercises

1. Cheyne-Stokes breathing is characterized by
   a) long, deep breaths through the nose and out the nose.
   b) fast, shallow breathing followed by slow, deep breathing.
   c) a gurgling noise caused by saliva in the throat.
   d) a rattling sound coming from the chest.

2. Thao is a 30-year-old client who is dying of cancer. Thao's family has been by their bedside for the last 3 days. Thao's mother takes you aside and explains that they wish the family to clean and dress Thao in their burial clothes after they die. You should
   a) report this to the nurse to get further directives.
   b) tell them that only staff can provide post-mortem care.
   c) ask why they wish the family to do their care.
   d) contact a representative of the family's faith.

3. When caring for a client who is dying, you should
   a) reposition the client every 2 hours.
   b) reposition the client every hour.
   c) provide oral care every 2–3 hours.
   d) use large comforters and blankets.

4. Edwin is an 86-year-old client who is dying of heart failure. Edwin's daughter is at their bedside. Edwin's daughter tells you that Edwin's breathing will stop for a minute before starting again. They are clearly upset by this. You should
   a) tell the daughter that you will start oxygen for their father.
   b) immediately report this to the nurse, as it is abnormal.
   c) reassure the daughter that apnea is a normal part of the dying process.
   d) ask the daughter to step out of the room.

5. Wanda is a 62-year-old who is dying of cancer. When you enter Wanda's room, you notice that they make a gurgling noise when they breathe. You should
   a) ask the nurse to suction Wanda's airways.
   b) do a finger-sweep and Heimlich maneuver.
   c) reposition Wanda and raise the head of the bed.
   d) start Wanda on oxygen for their comfort.

6. Cora is dying of emphysema. Cora's oxygen is on at 3L per minute via nasal cannula. Their son tells you that Cora has been trying to take their oxygen off. Cora says they don't want to wear it anymore, but the son is insisting that Cora keep the oxygen on. You should
   a) tell Cora that they need to keep their oxygen on.
   b) tell Cora's son that this is a normal part of the dying process.
   c) put Cora's oxygen back on using an oxygen mask.
   d) update the nurse and wait for directives.

7. Bertha's family has been at their bedside for the last 5 days. As you approach Bertha's room, you hear loud, angry voices. You discover two of Bertha's daughters arguing with each other. You should
   a) remain outside the room to allow them privacy.
   b) politely intervene and encourage them to go for a walk.
   c) report the incident to the facility's social worker.
   d) tell them that their arguing will just upset their mother.

8. When providing post-mortem care, the nursing assistant is responsible for all of the following EXCEPT

   a) bathing the client's body.
   b) putting the client's dentures in.
   c) listening for a heartbeat.
   d) tidying the client's room.

9. The first stage of grief is typically

   a) bargaining.
   b) denial.
   c) depression.
   d) anger.

26.E Choose the best response to the following scenarios.

1. The family is in the room of a client you are caring for. The client is dying, and the family members are talking about the client like they have already passed away. What should you do?

   a) Tell the family that they are being rude.
   b) Set a good example by speaking to the client while caring for them.
   c) Read the family the dying client's bill of rights.
   d) Turn up the television so that the client can't hear this.

2. Your dying client asks you to say the Lord's Prayer with them, but you don't know it. What should you do?

   a) Offer to hold the client's hand while they say the prayer.
   b) Explain to the client that you are not Catholic.
   c) Search for the prayer on your cell phone and then pray with them.
   d) Ask the client to wait until the priest arrives.

3. You are taking care of a client who is dying. They tell you that they are seeing beautiful butterflies and angels in the room. What should you do?

   a) Tell them that they are having a hallucination and that it is a normal part of dying.
   b) Leave the client alone and then report this to the family.
   c) Ask the client to explain what they are seeing.
   d) Turn on the television while you are caregiving to distract them.

4. Your client has died, and it is your responsibility to perform post-mortem care. You have never done this and are nervous. What should you do?

   a) Ask for assistance from another nursing assistant and remain professional.
   b) Refuse to care for the client because it makes you uncomfortable.
   c) Care for the client based on what you remember from your class.
   d) Inform the nurse that this is not in your scope of practice.

5. Your client passed away last night. The family calls to say they would like to pack up their loved one's personal belongings. What should you do?

   a) Try to avoid them so you don't make them upset.
   b) Have the belongings packed for them and waiting at the nurse's desk.
   c) Pack up the belongings with the family members, reminding them that they will feel better soon.
   d) Tell them that you are sorry for their loss and then allow them to pack their loved one's belongings.